CREATE AND RELAX
Coloring Activities
And More

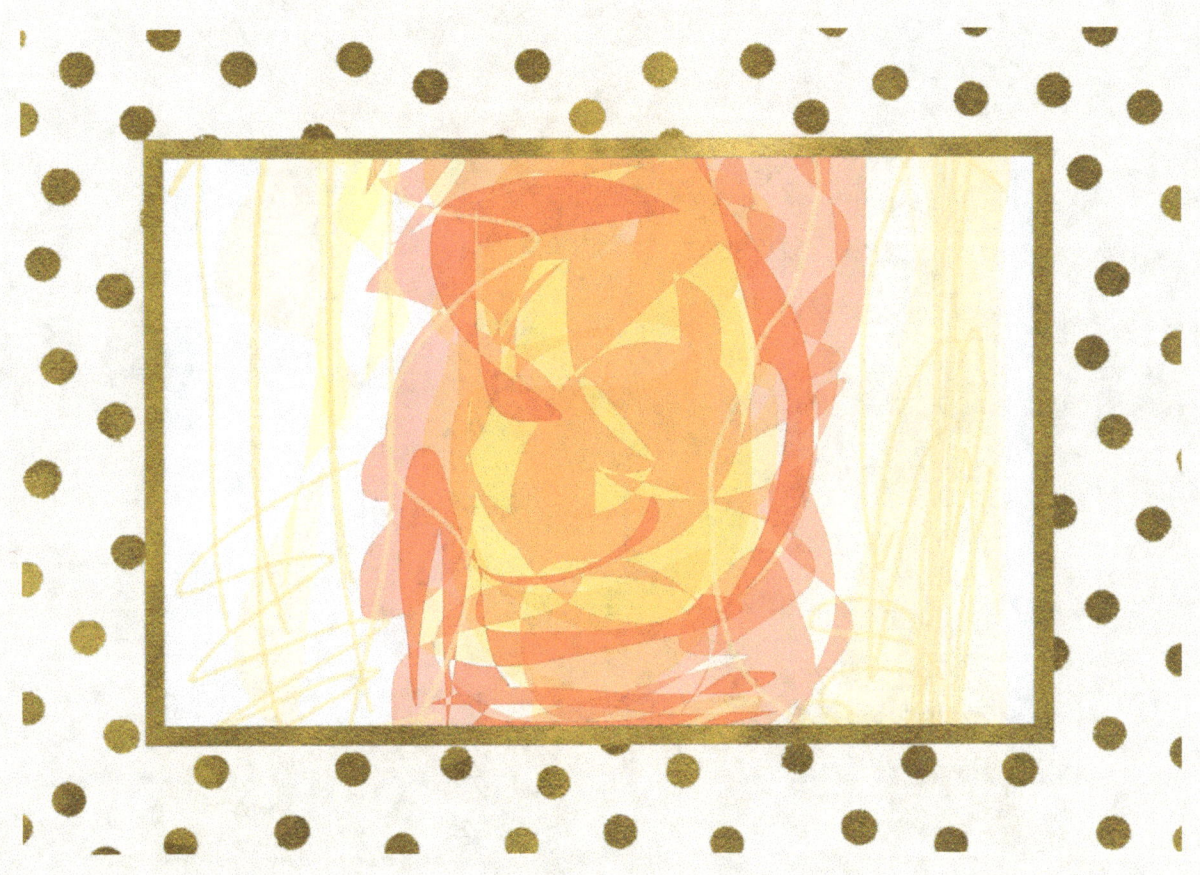

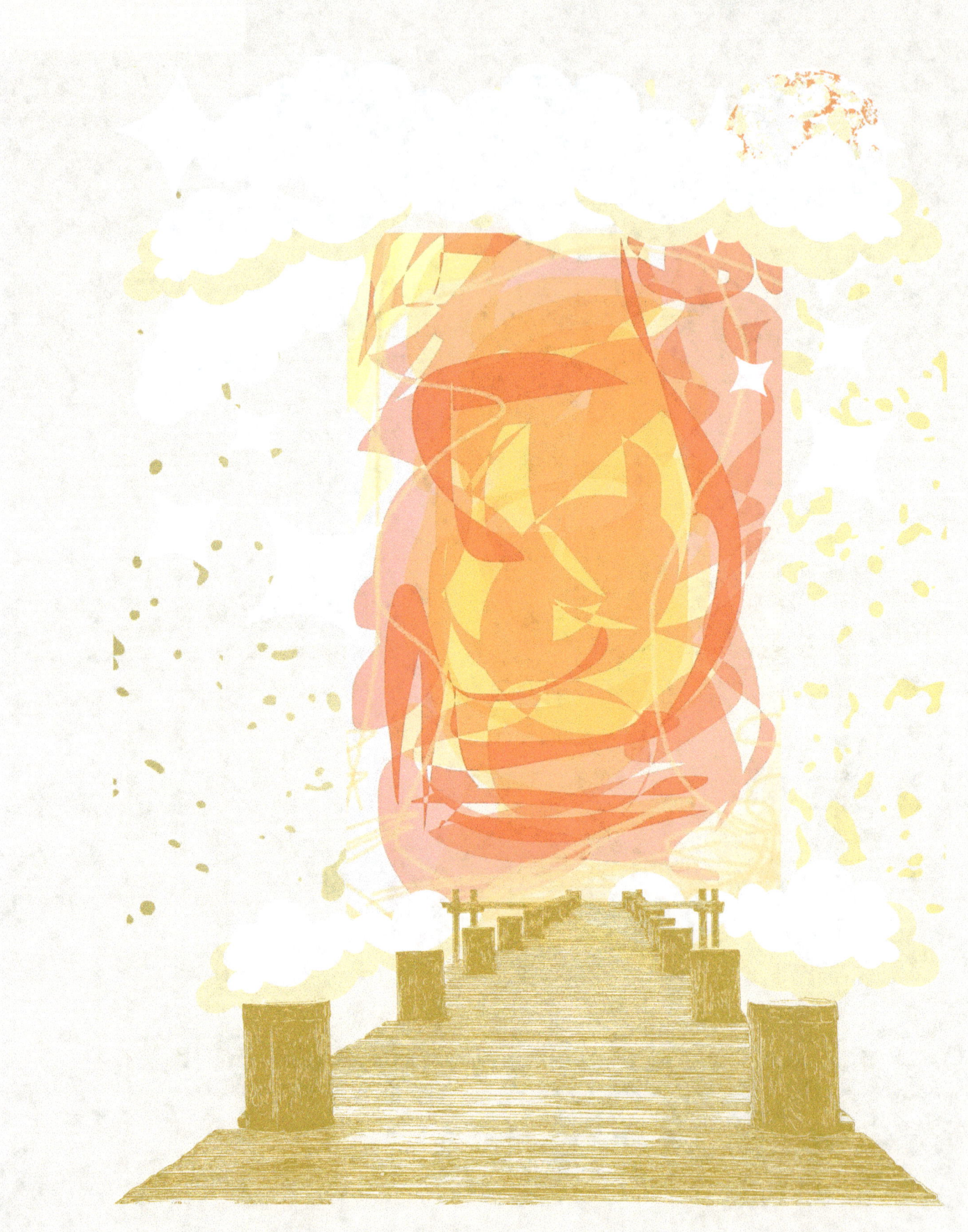

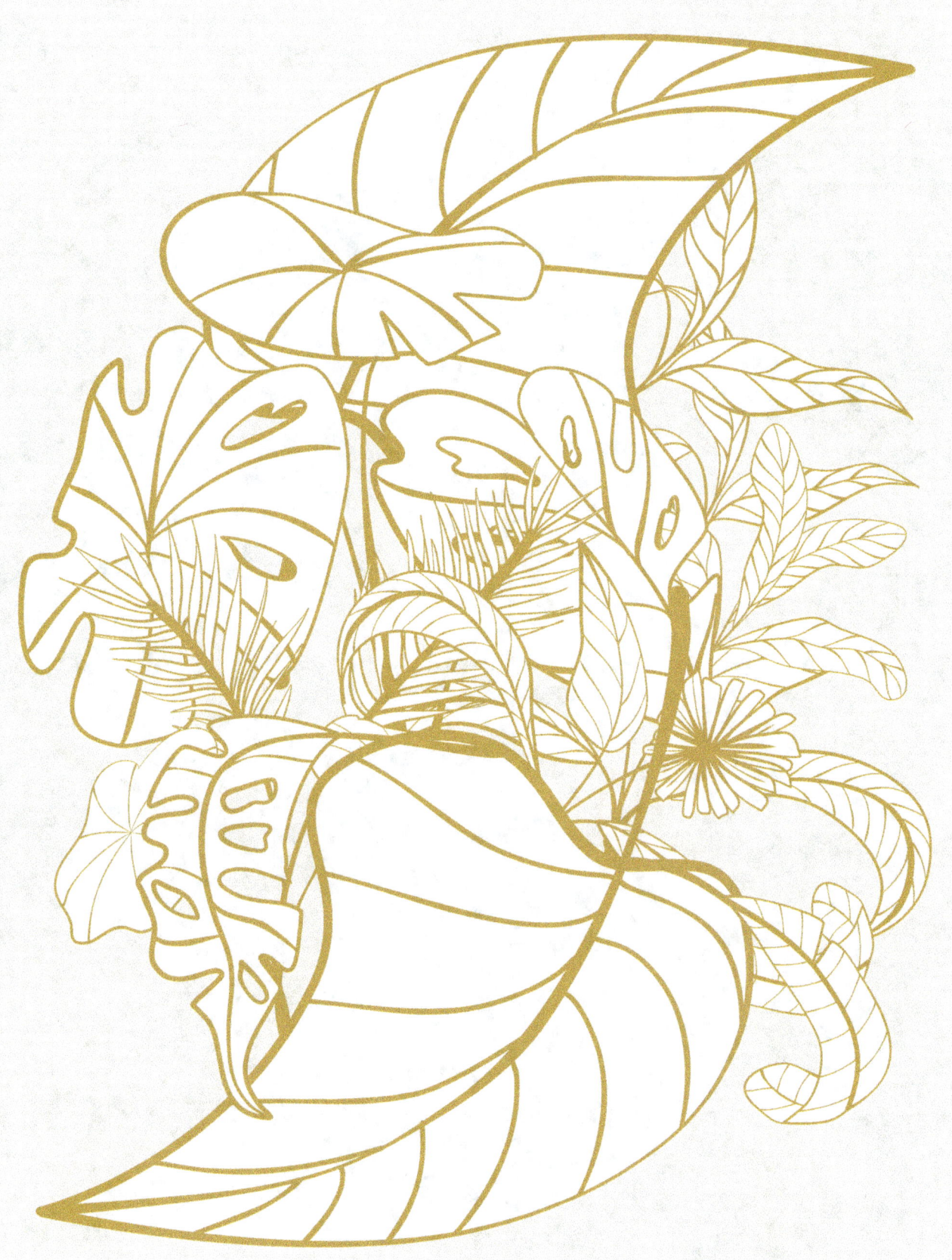

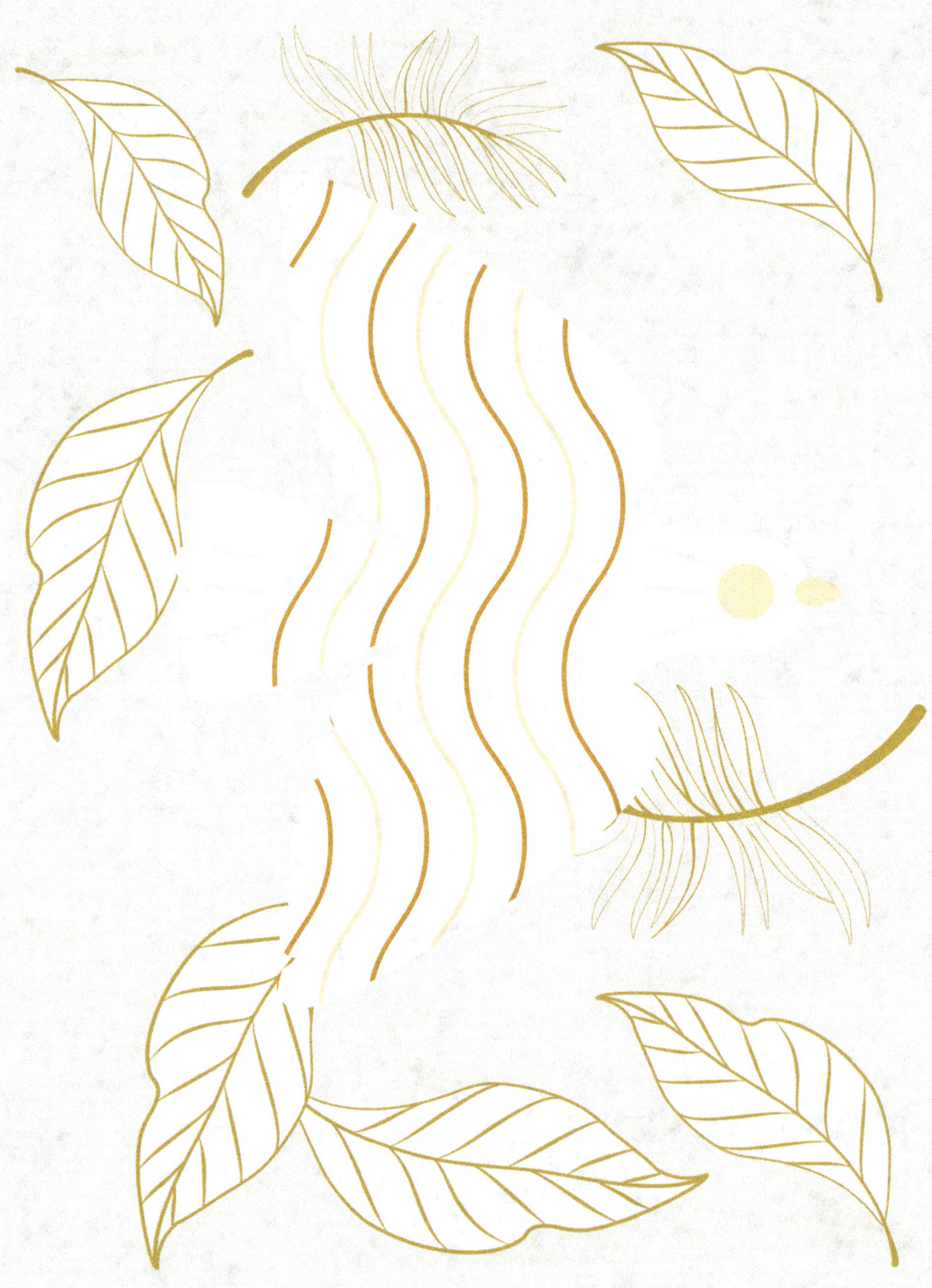

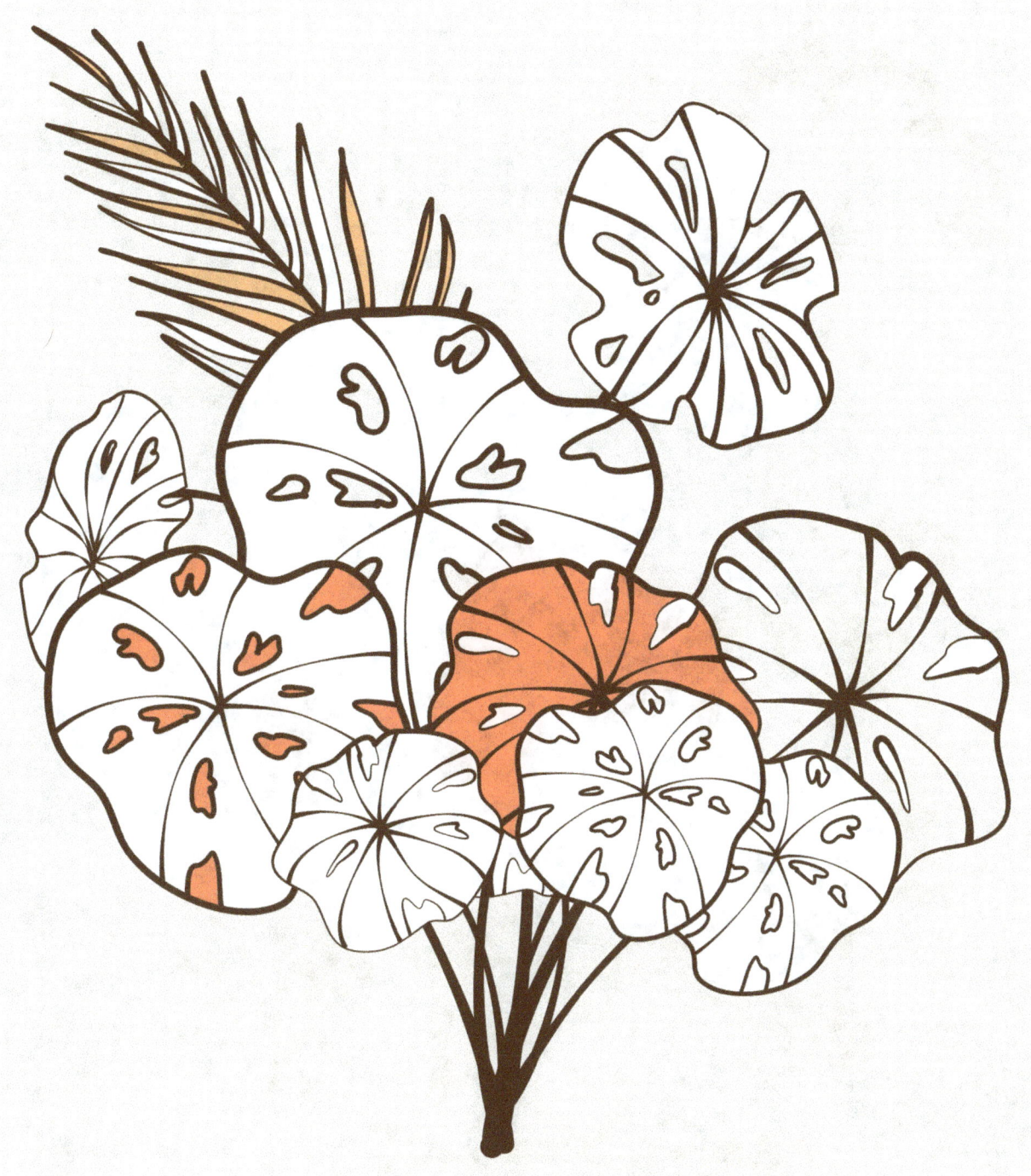

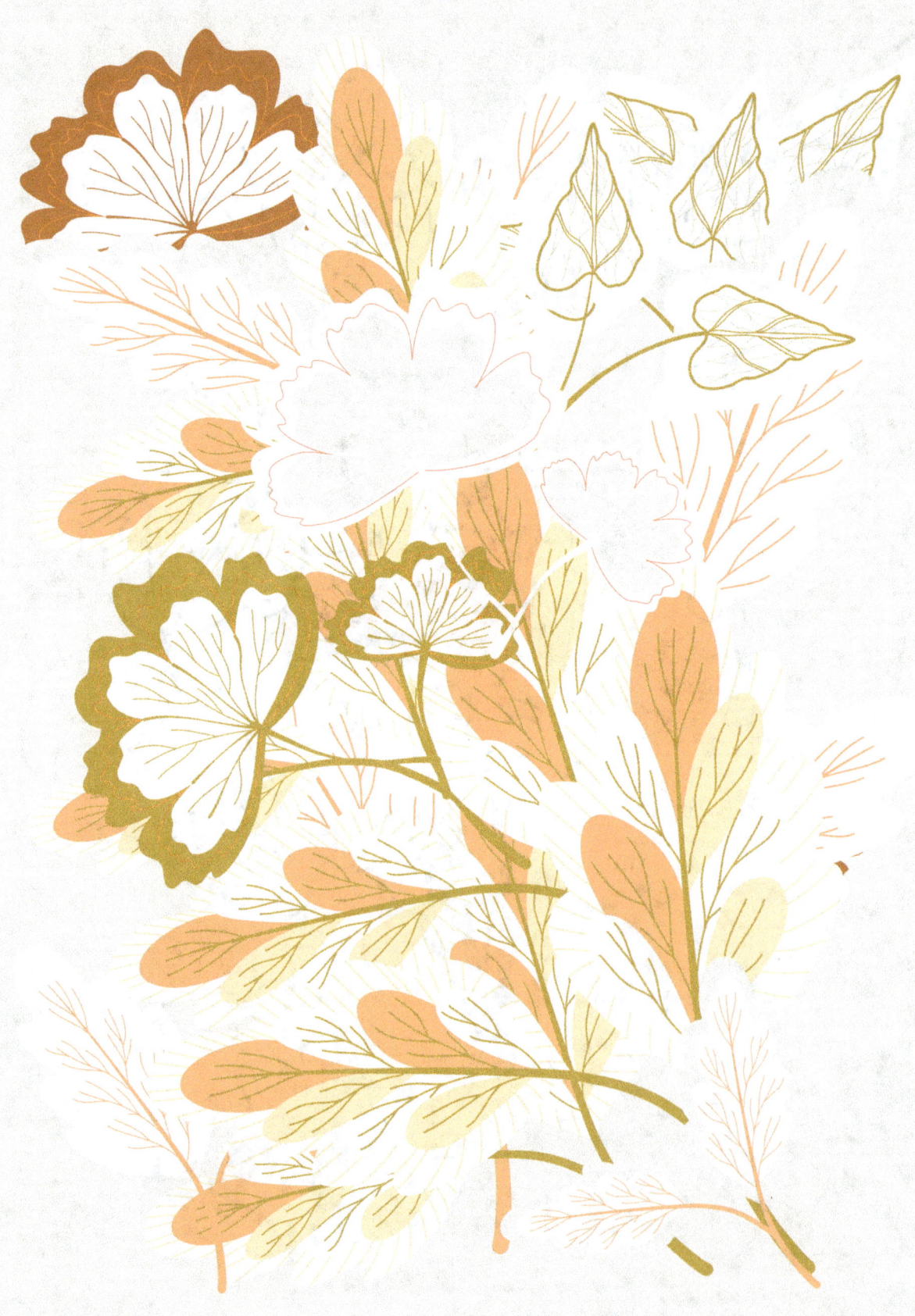

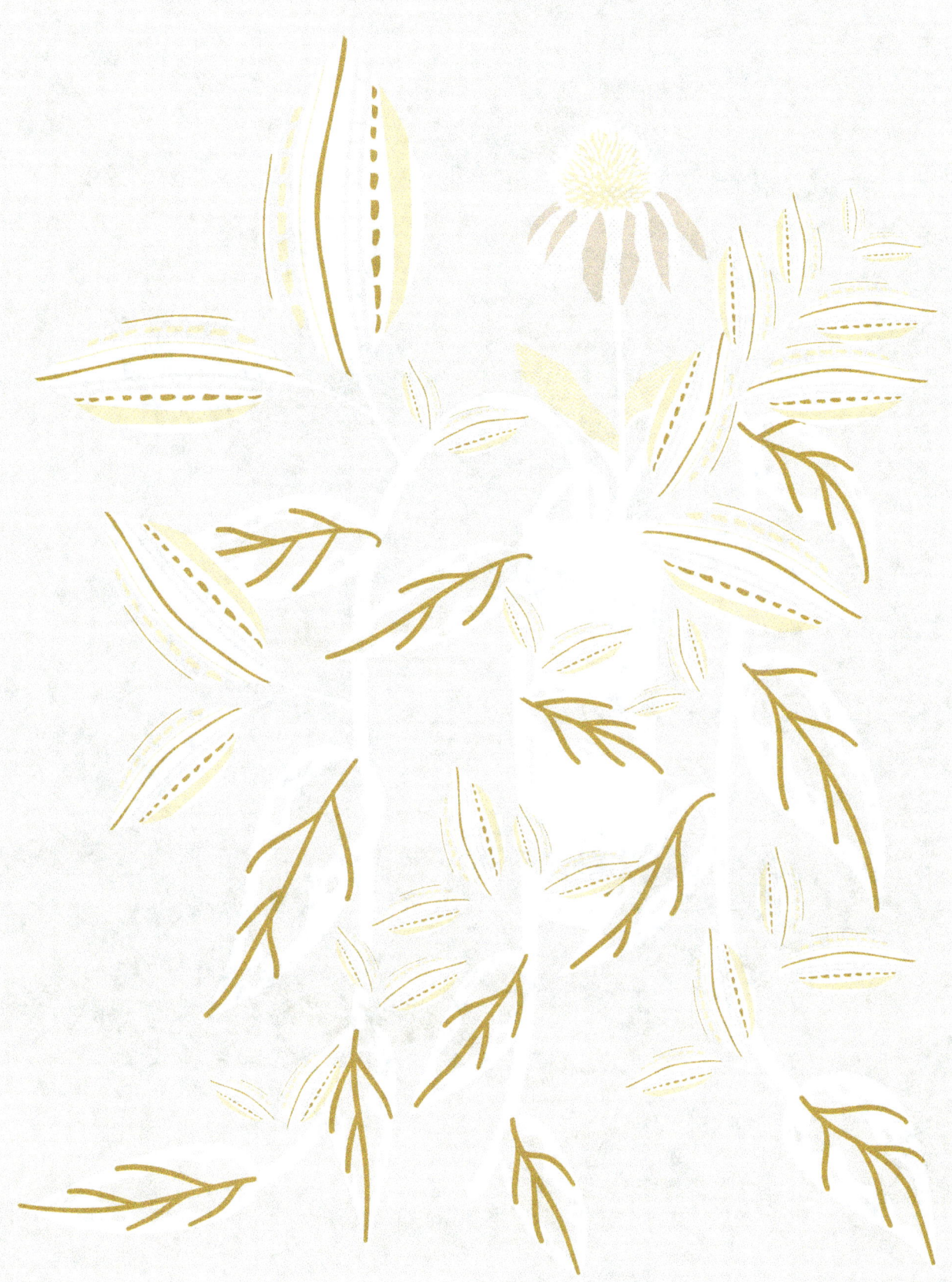

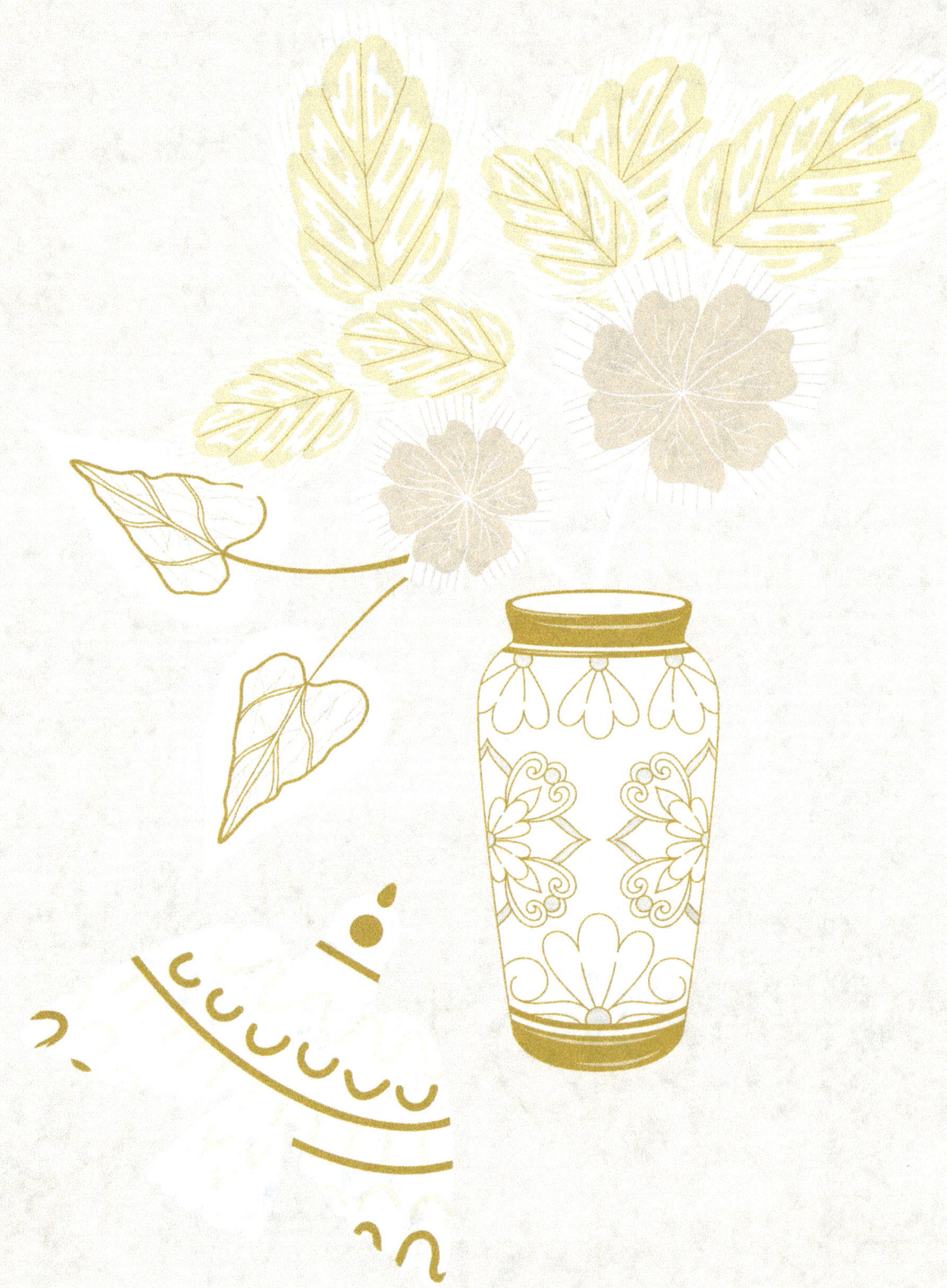

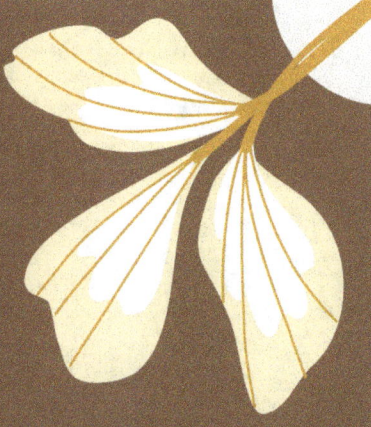

Love To Create

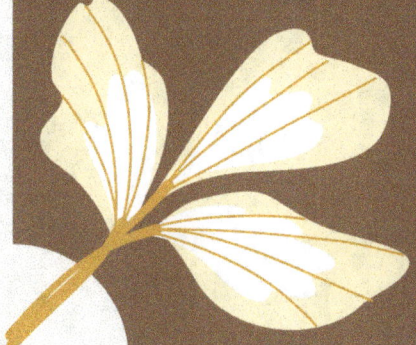

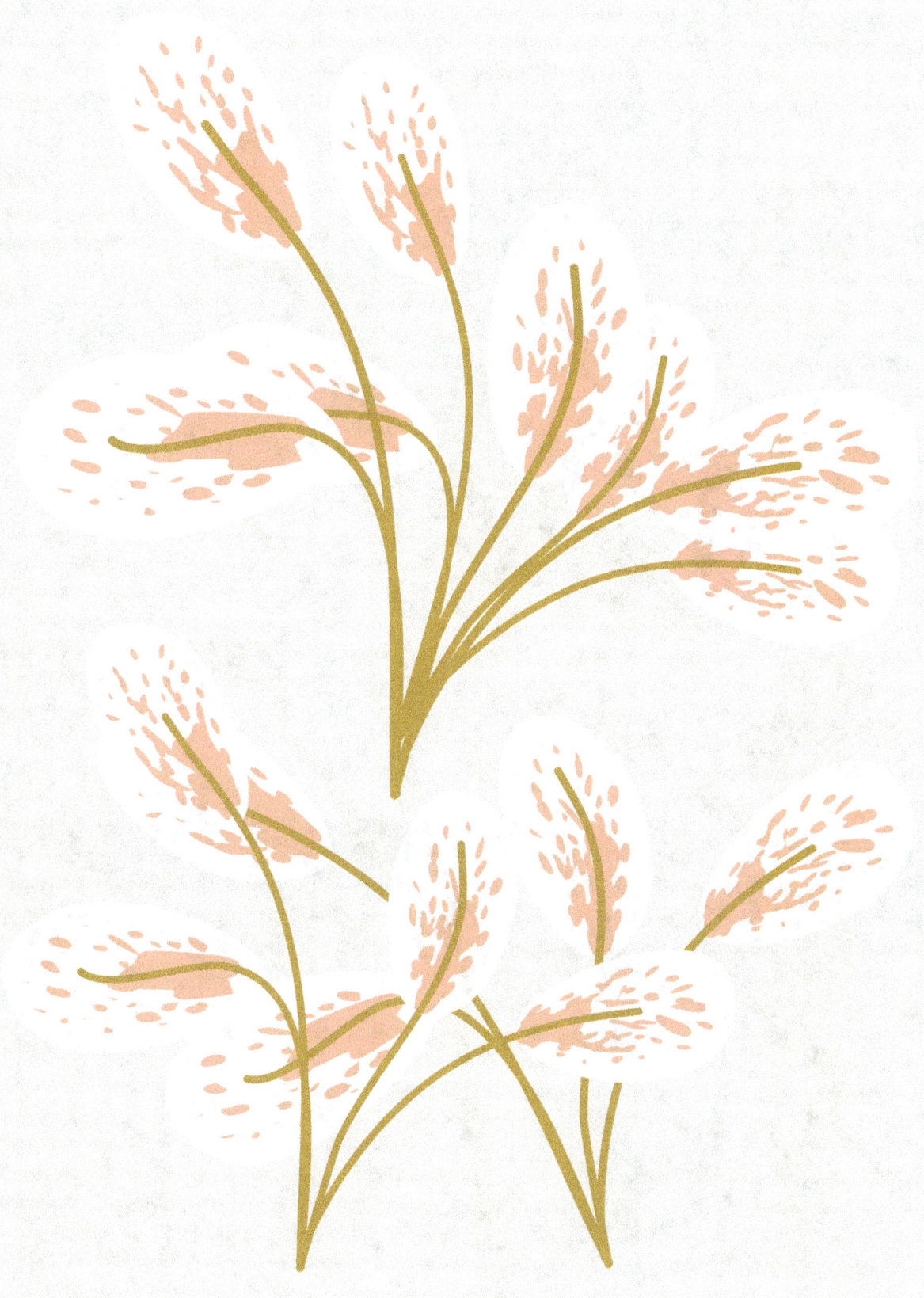

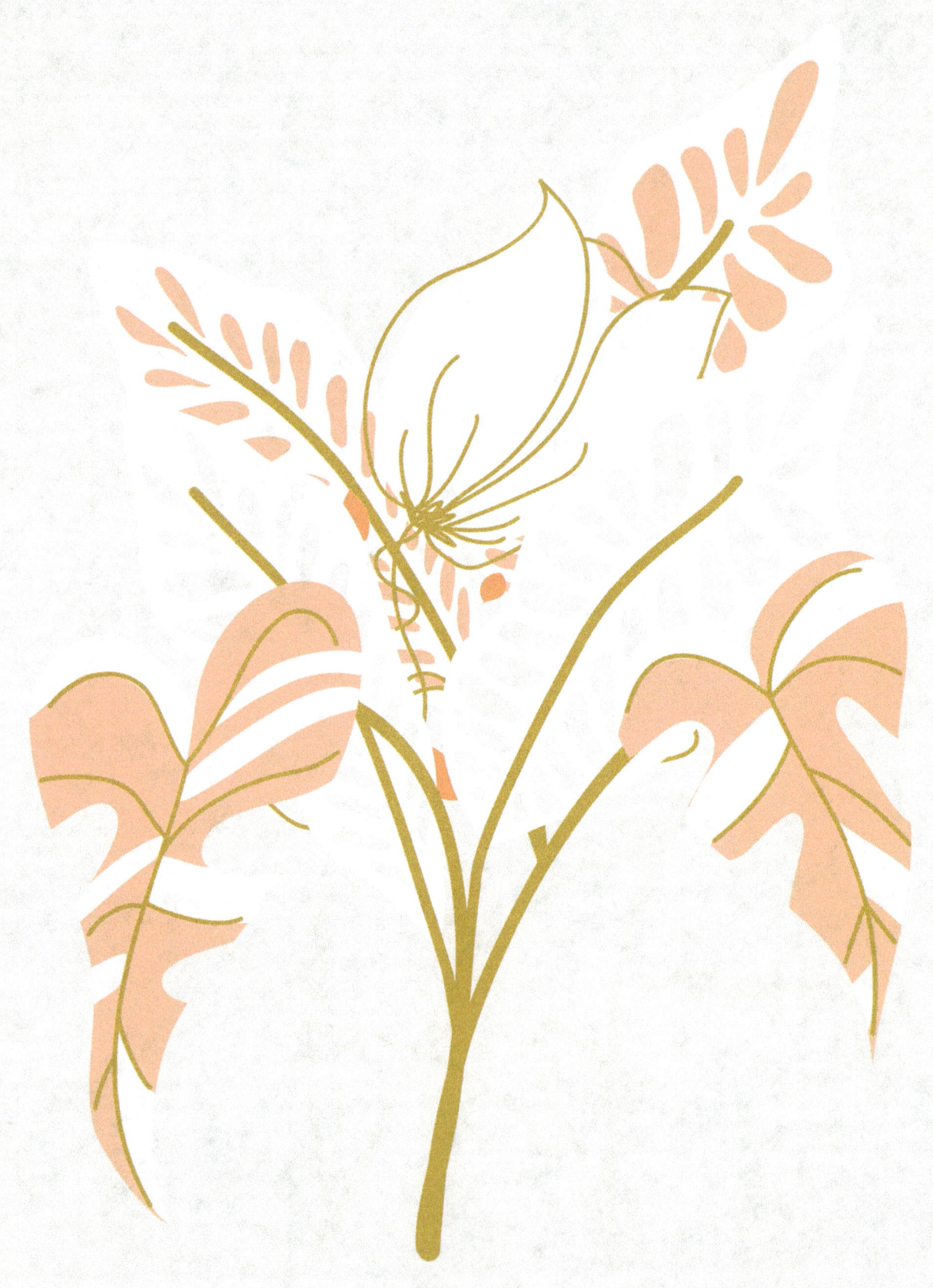

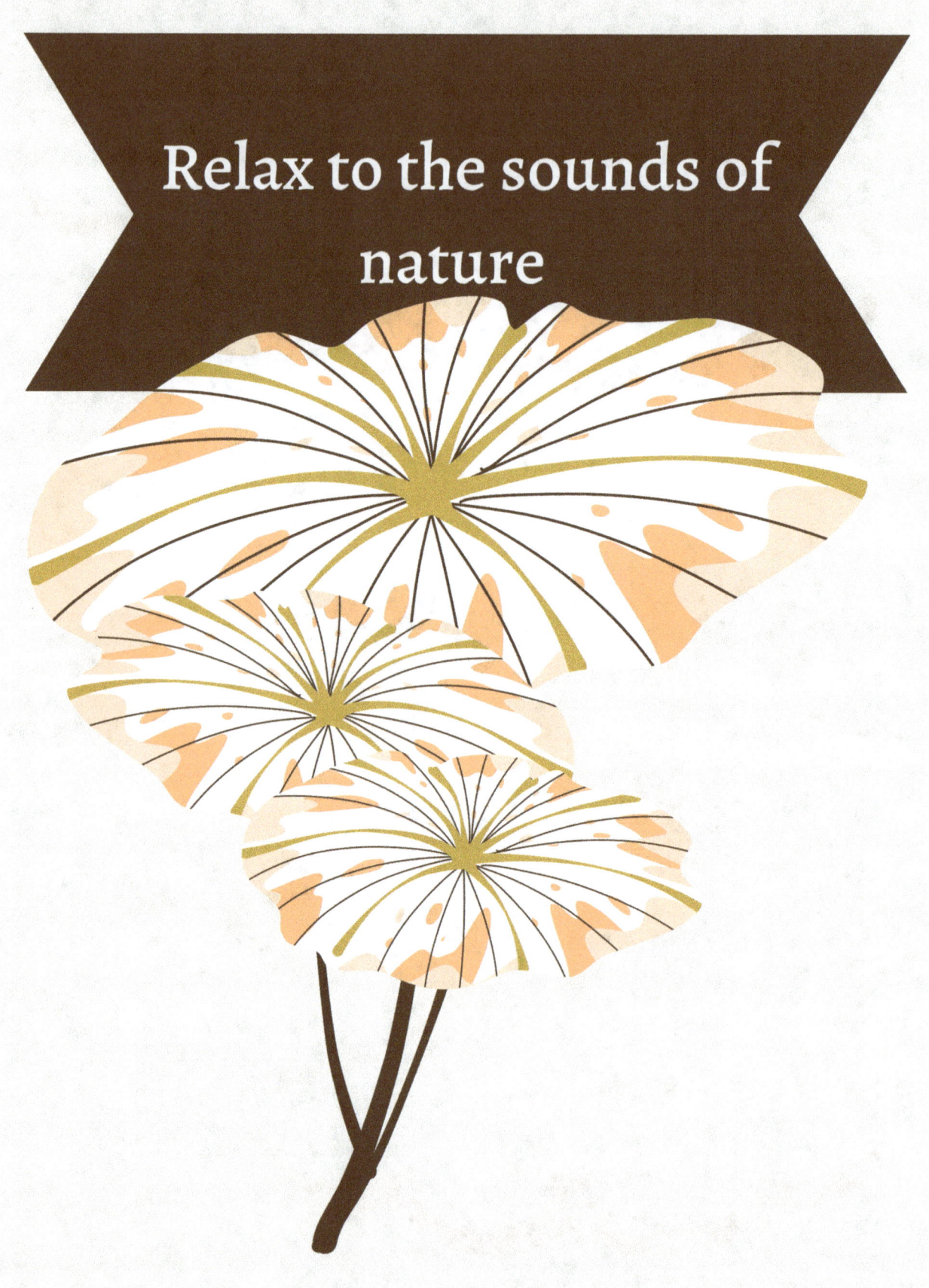

Relax to the sounds of nature

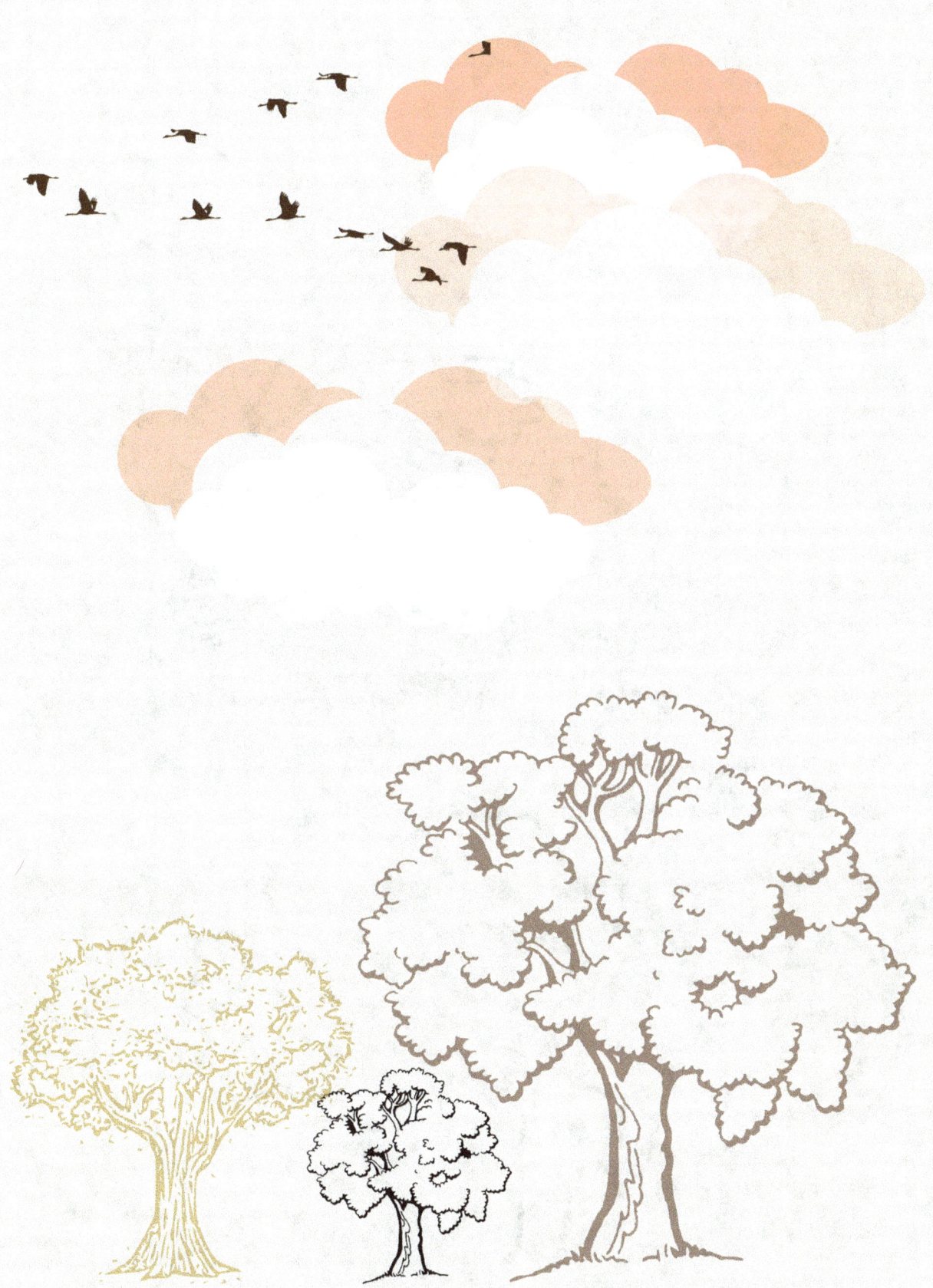

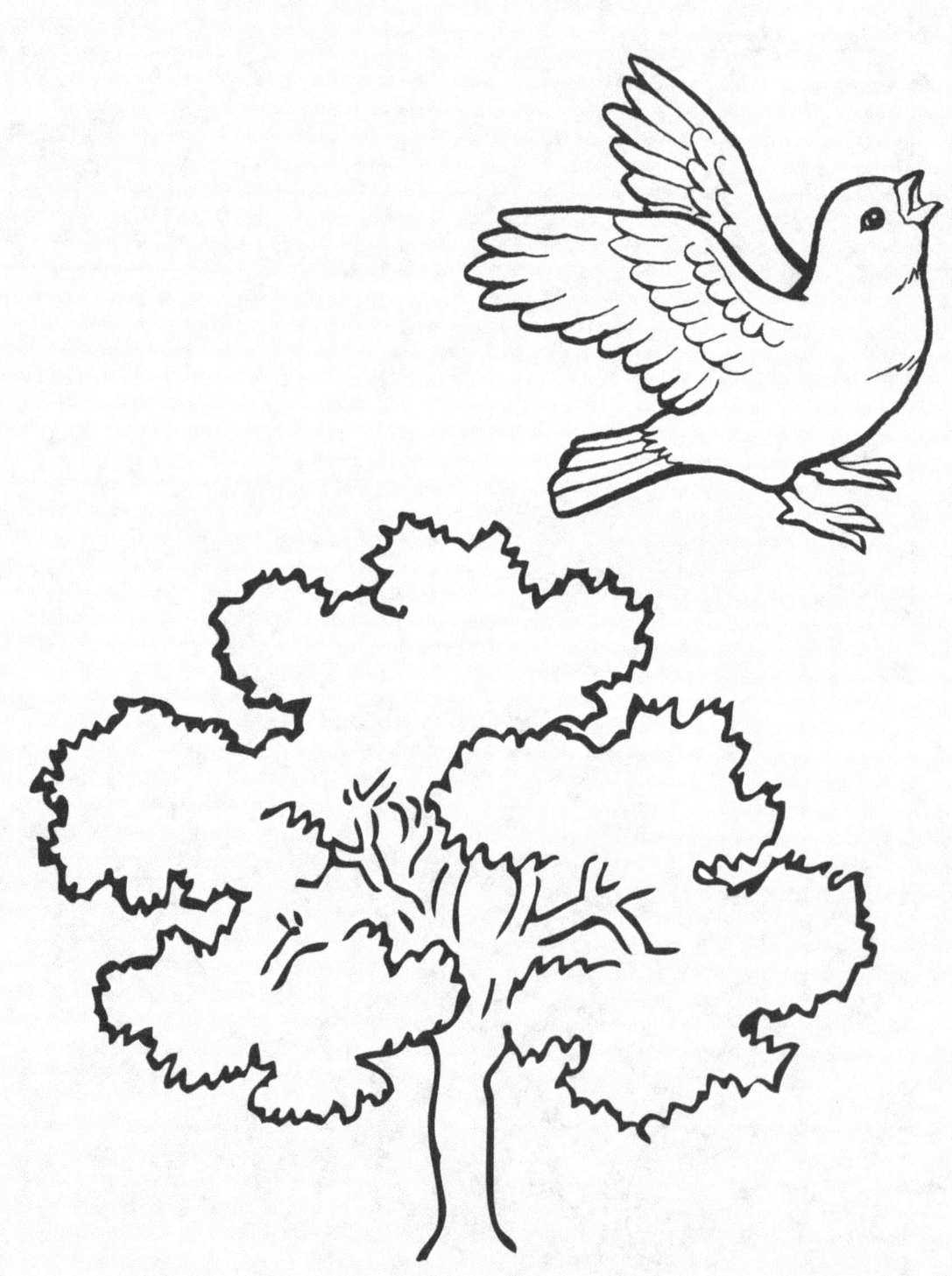

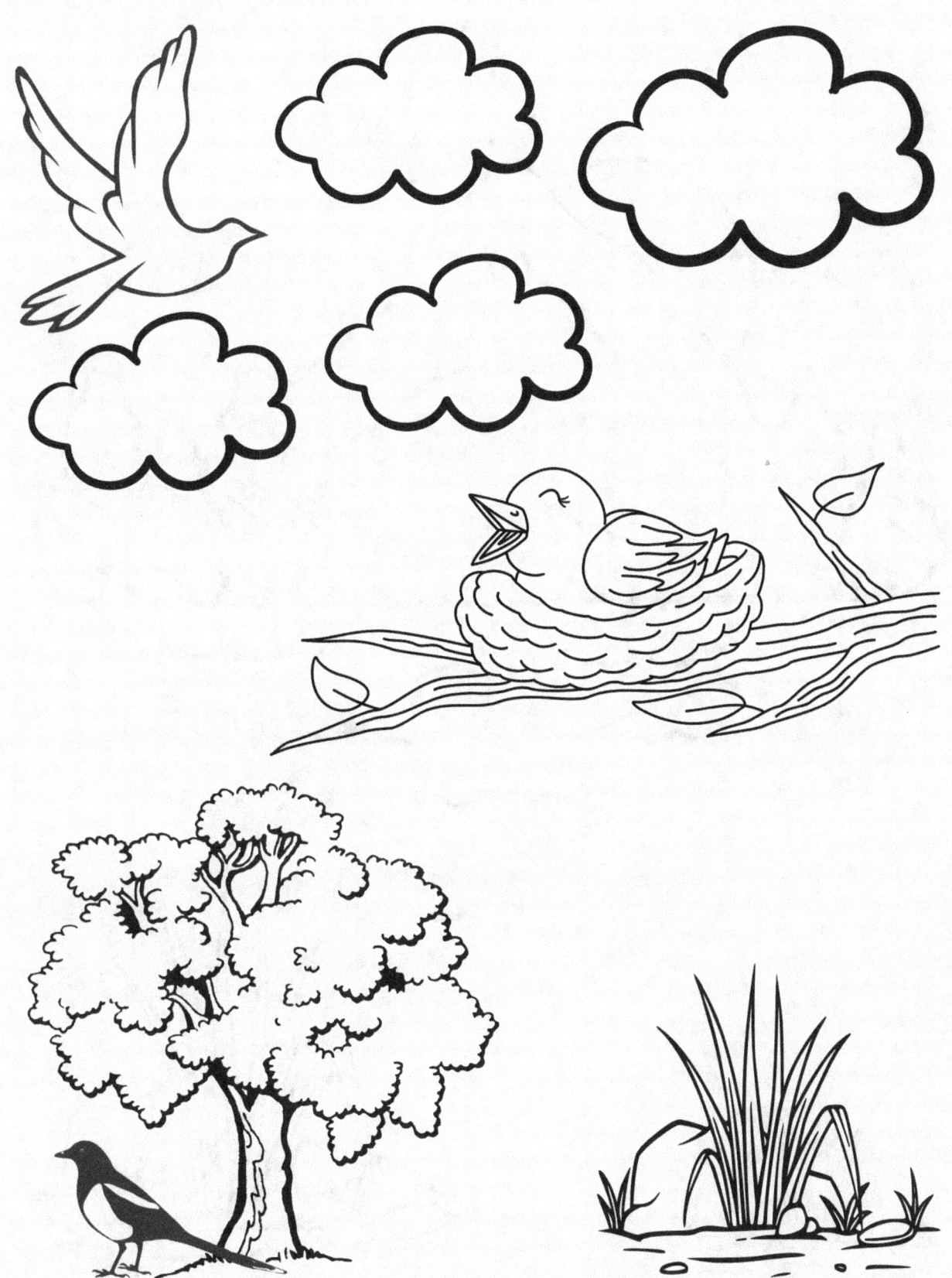

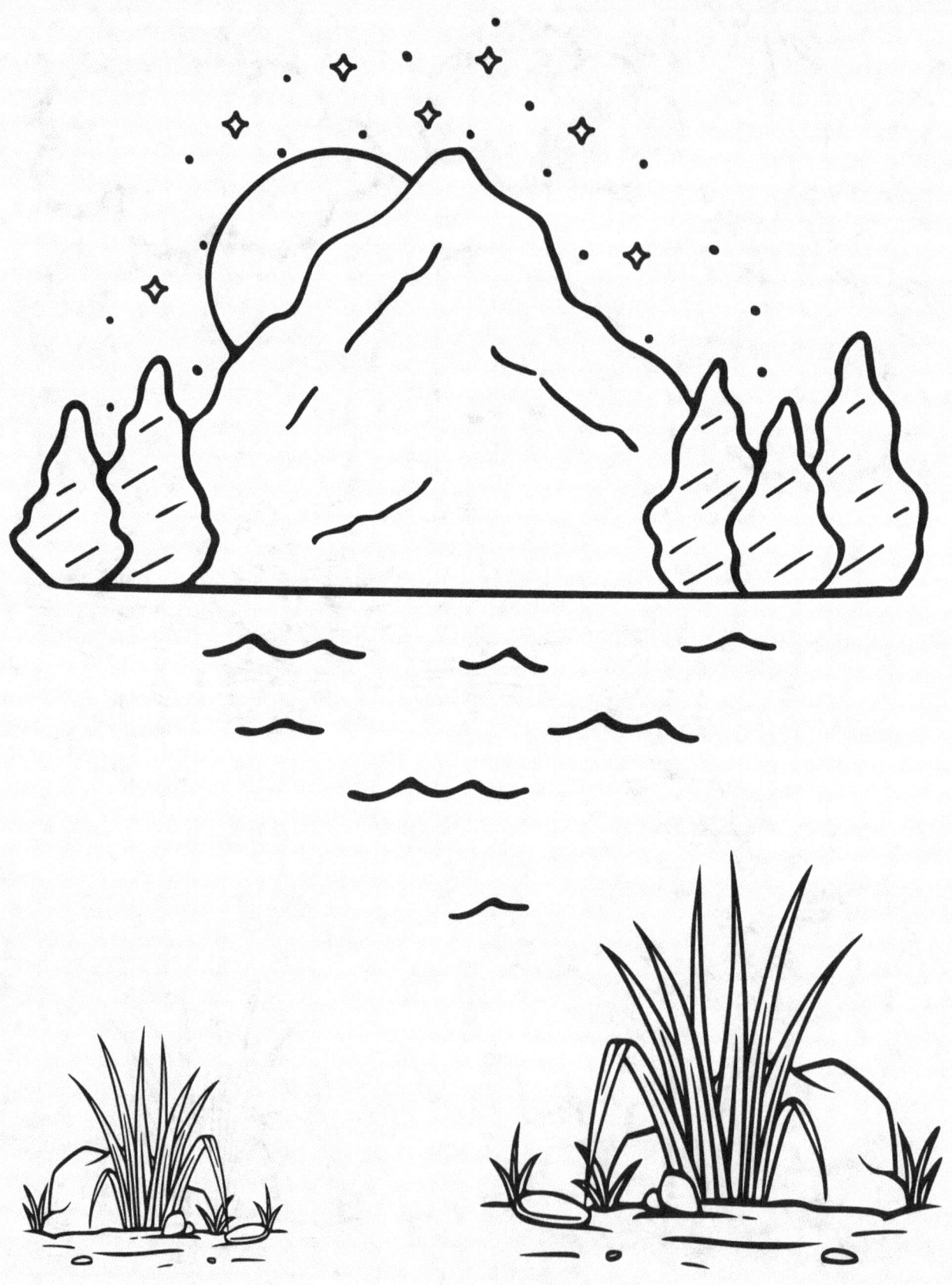

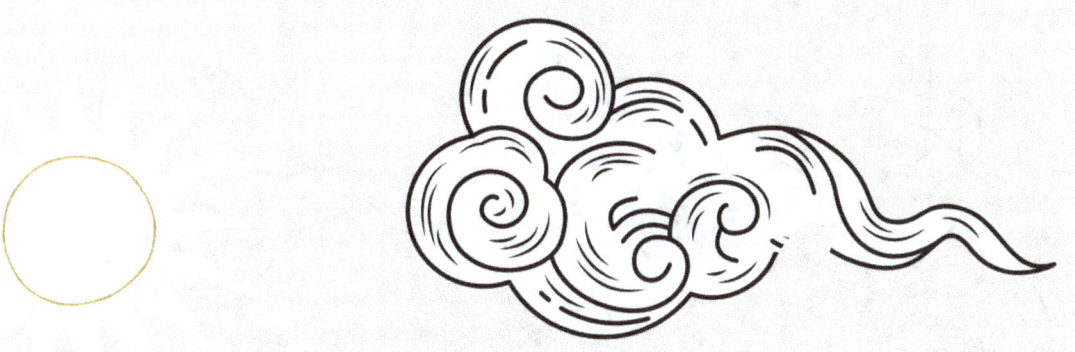
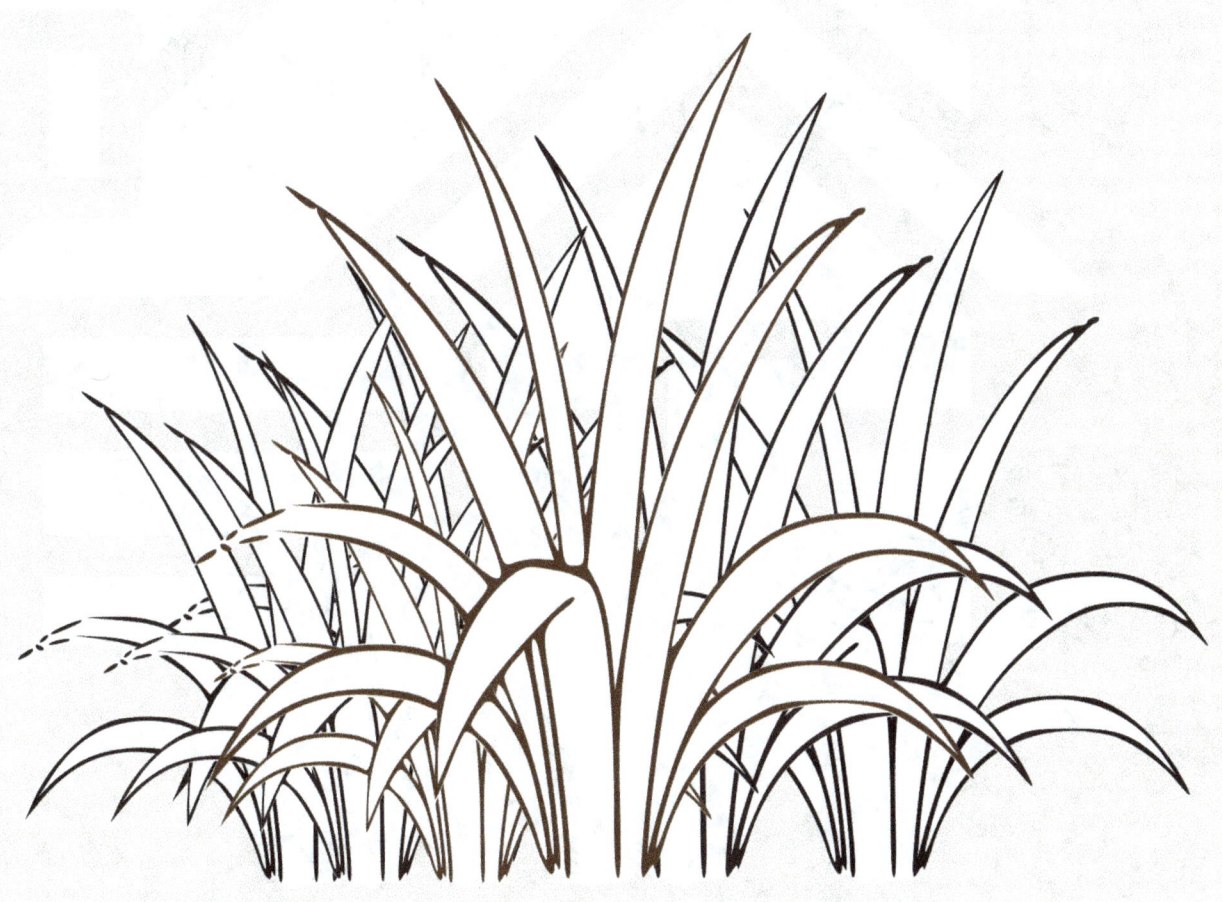

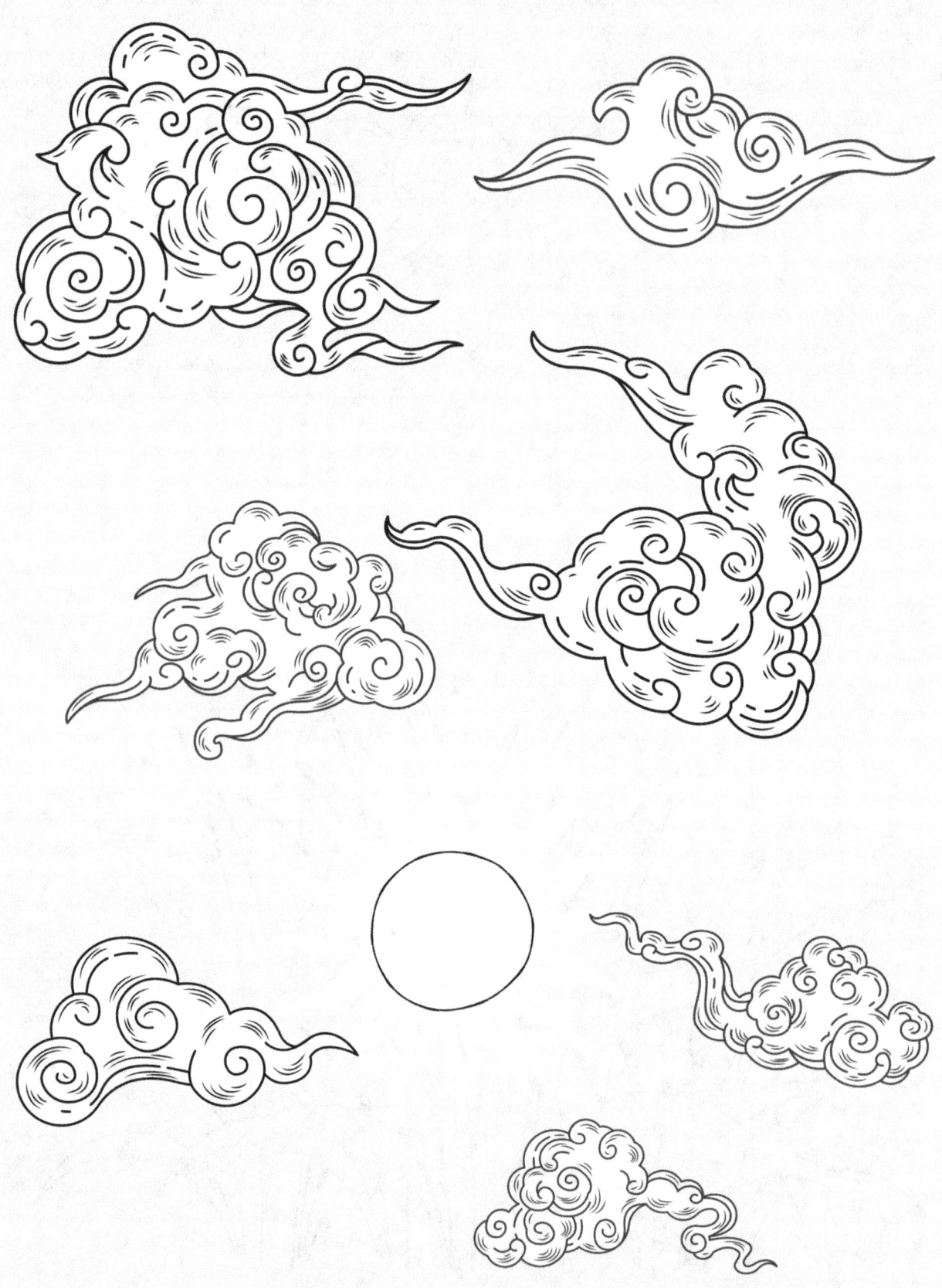

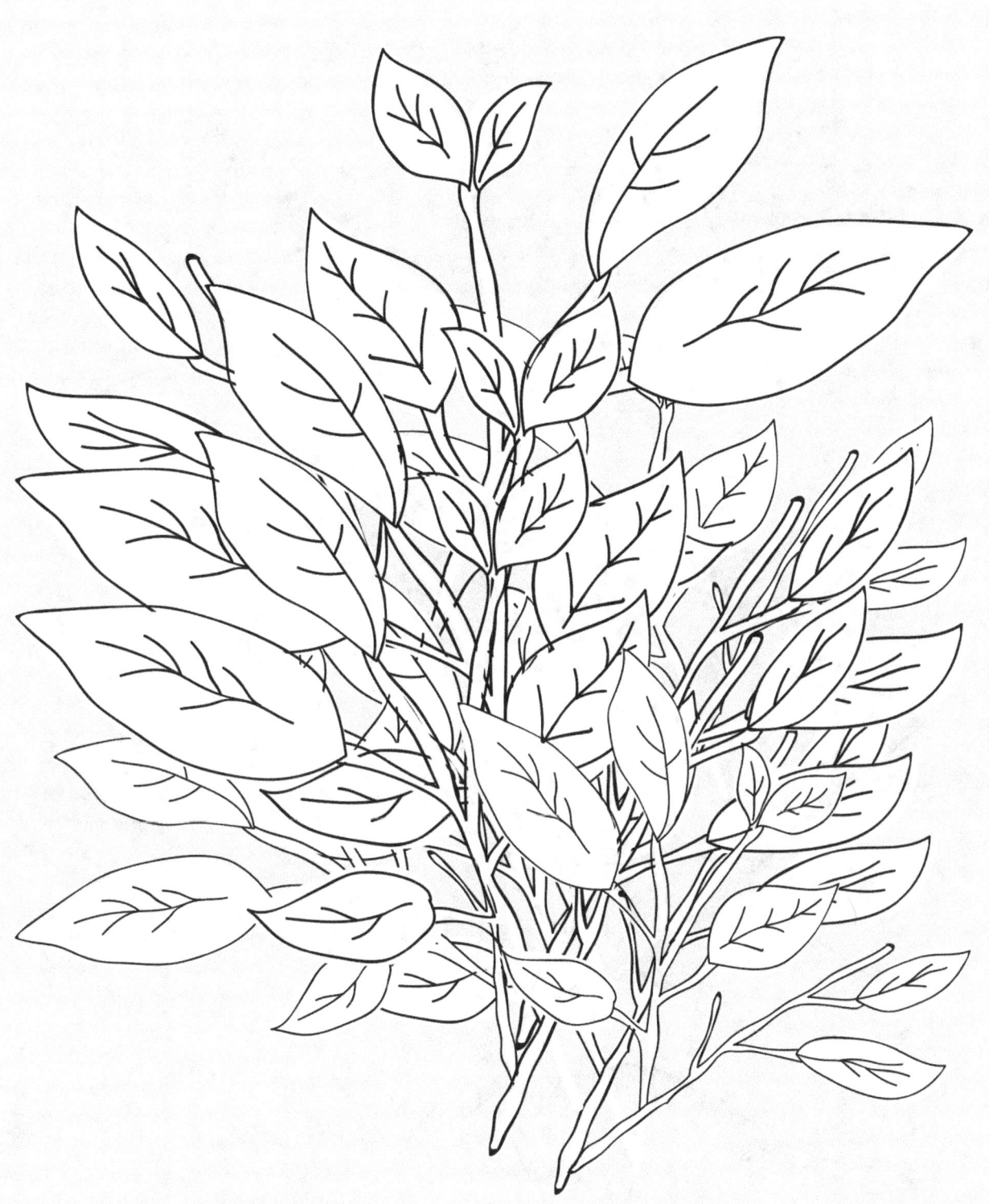

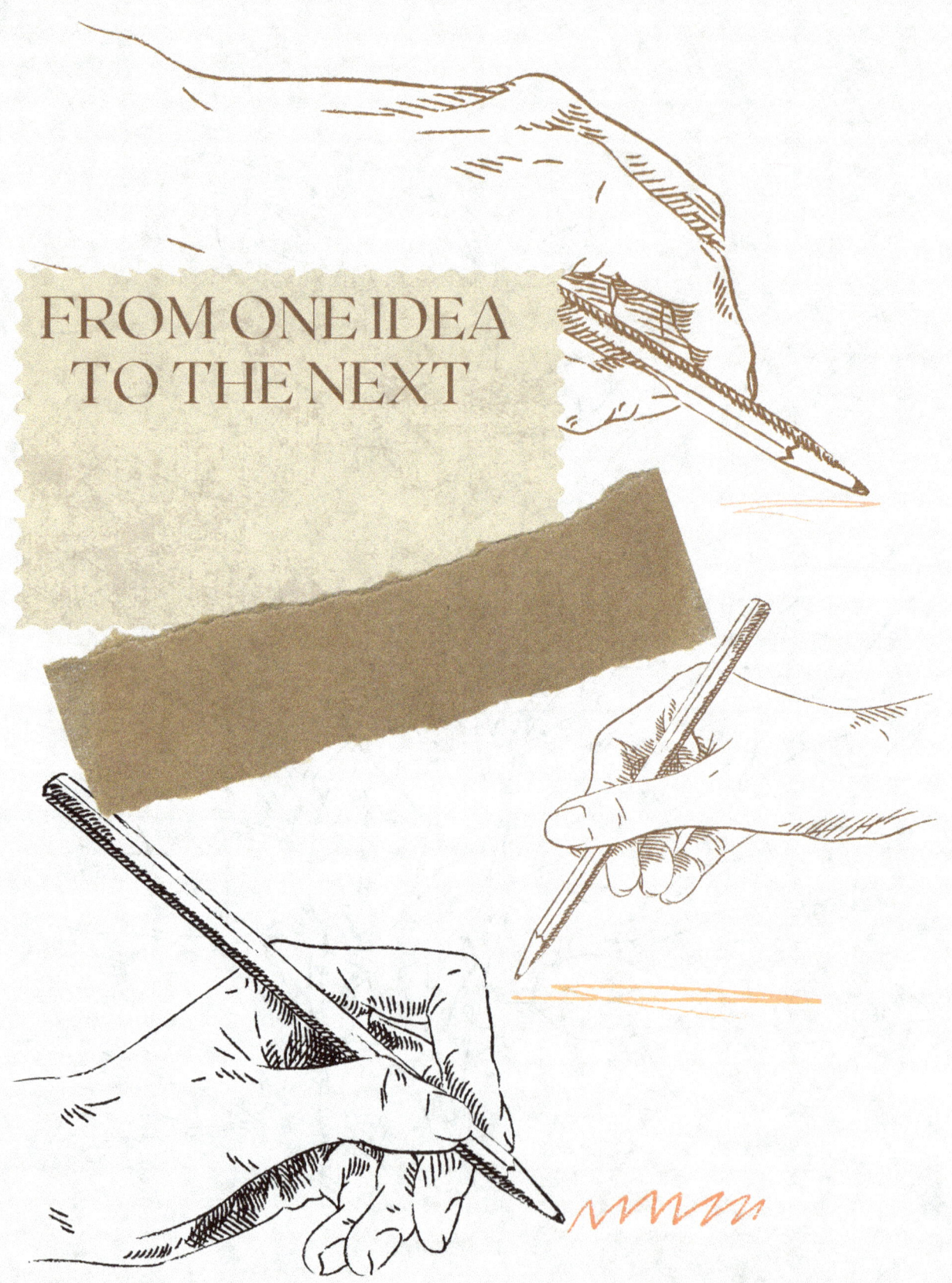

FROM ONE IDEA
TO THE NEXT

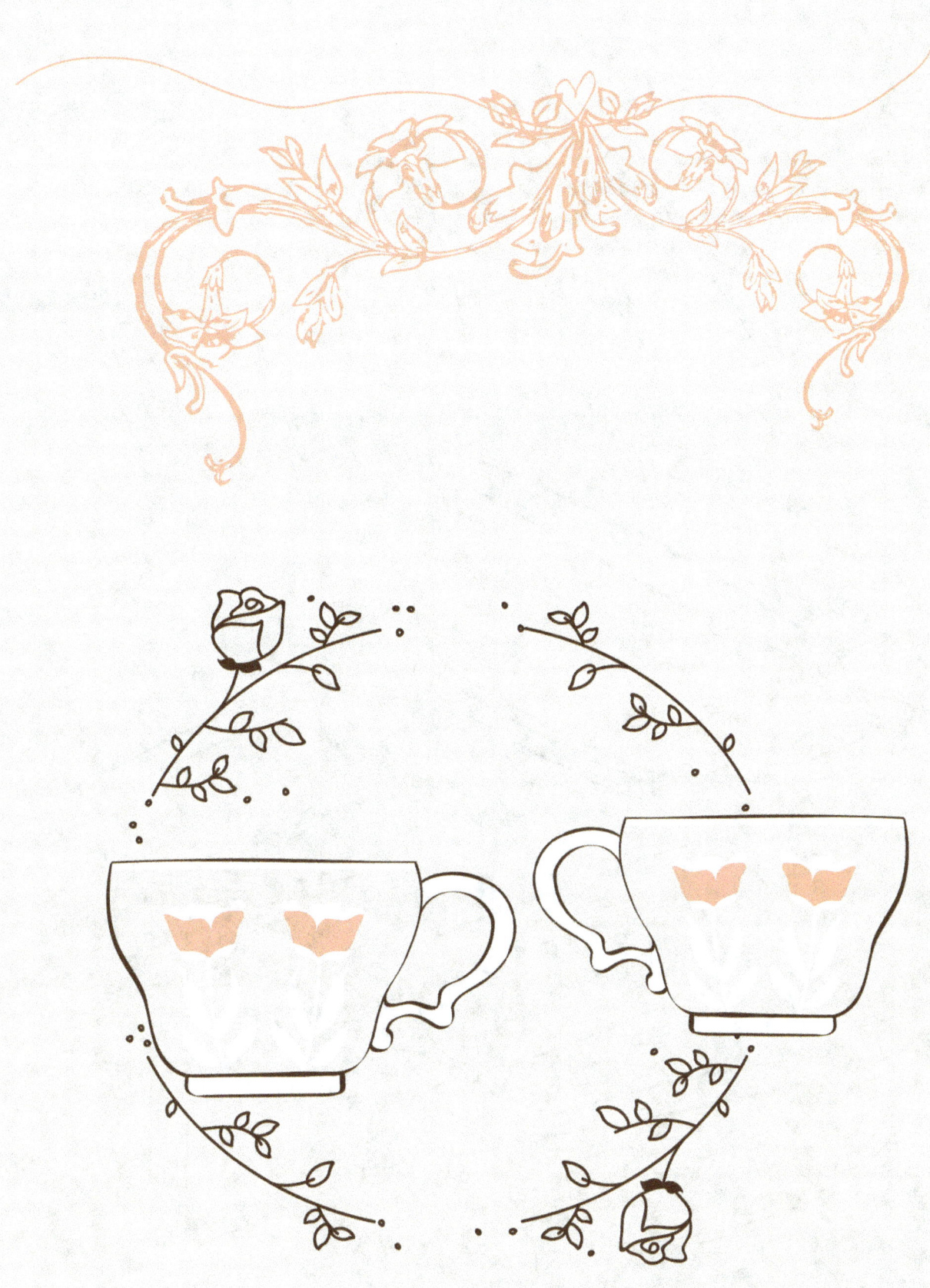

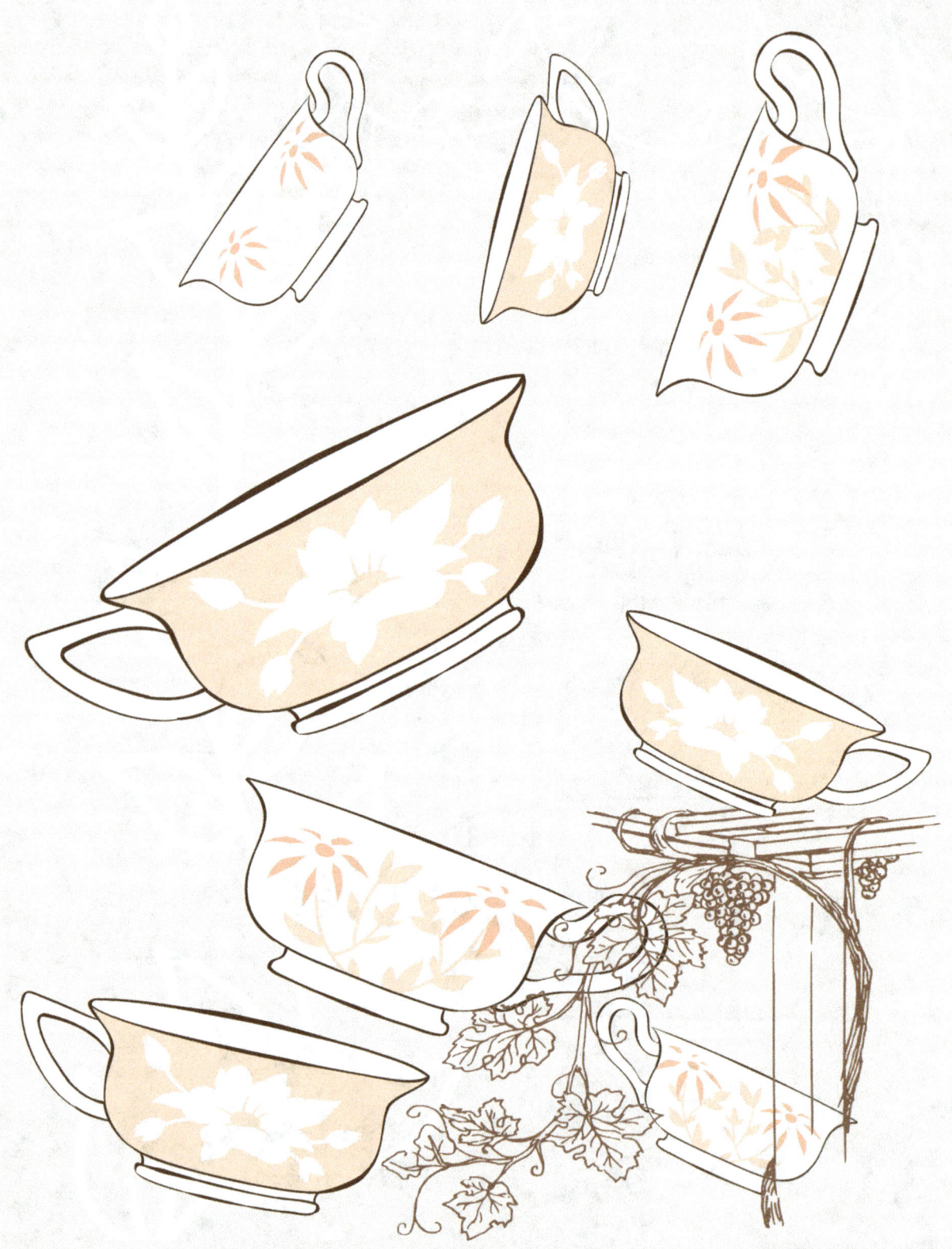

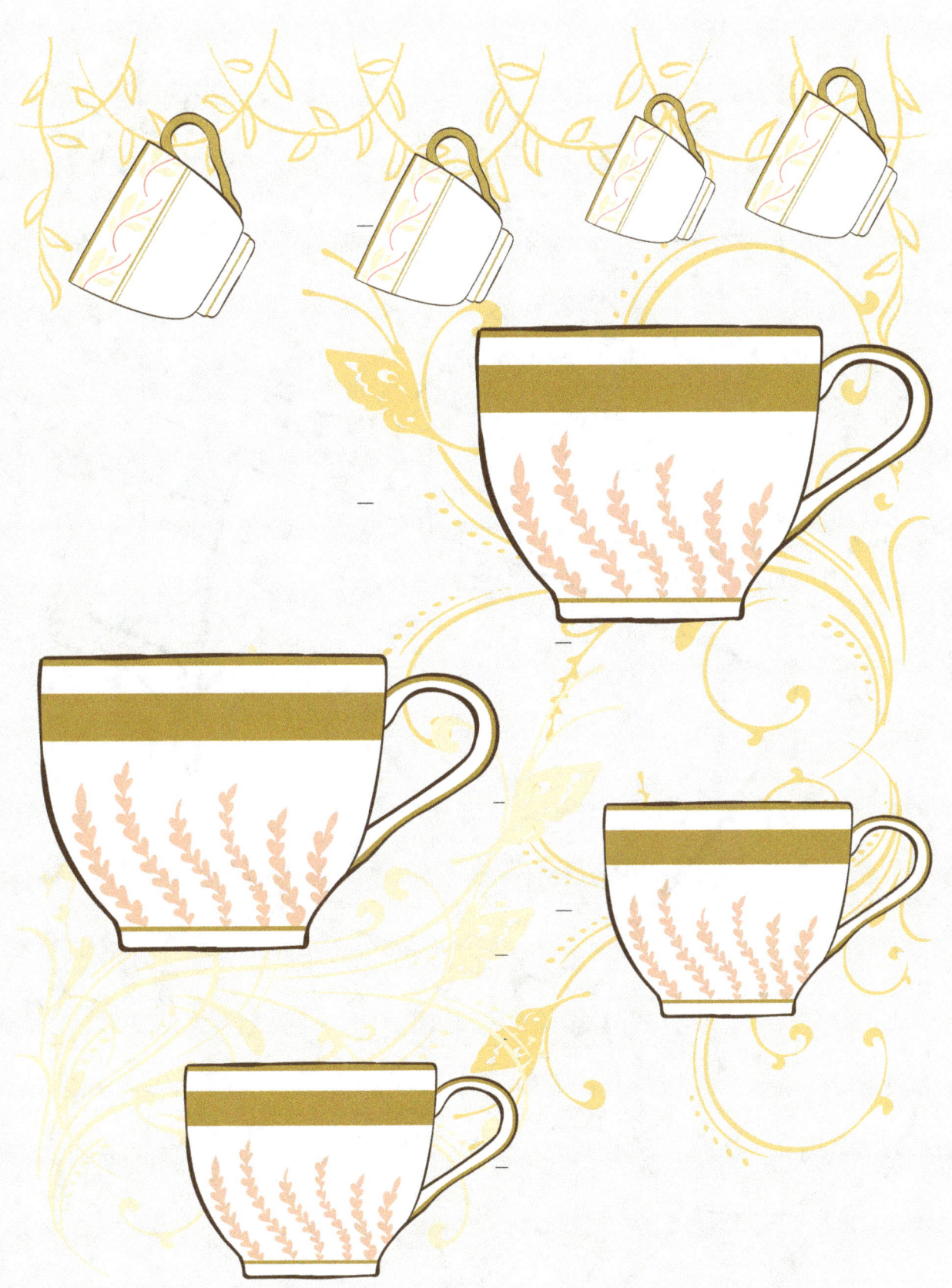

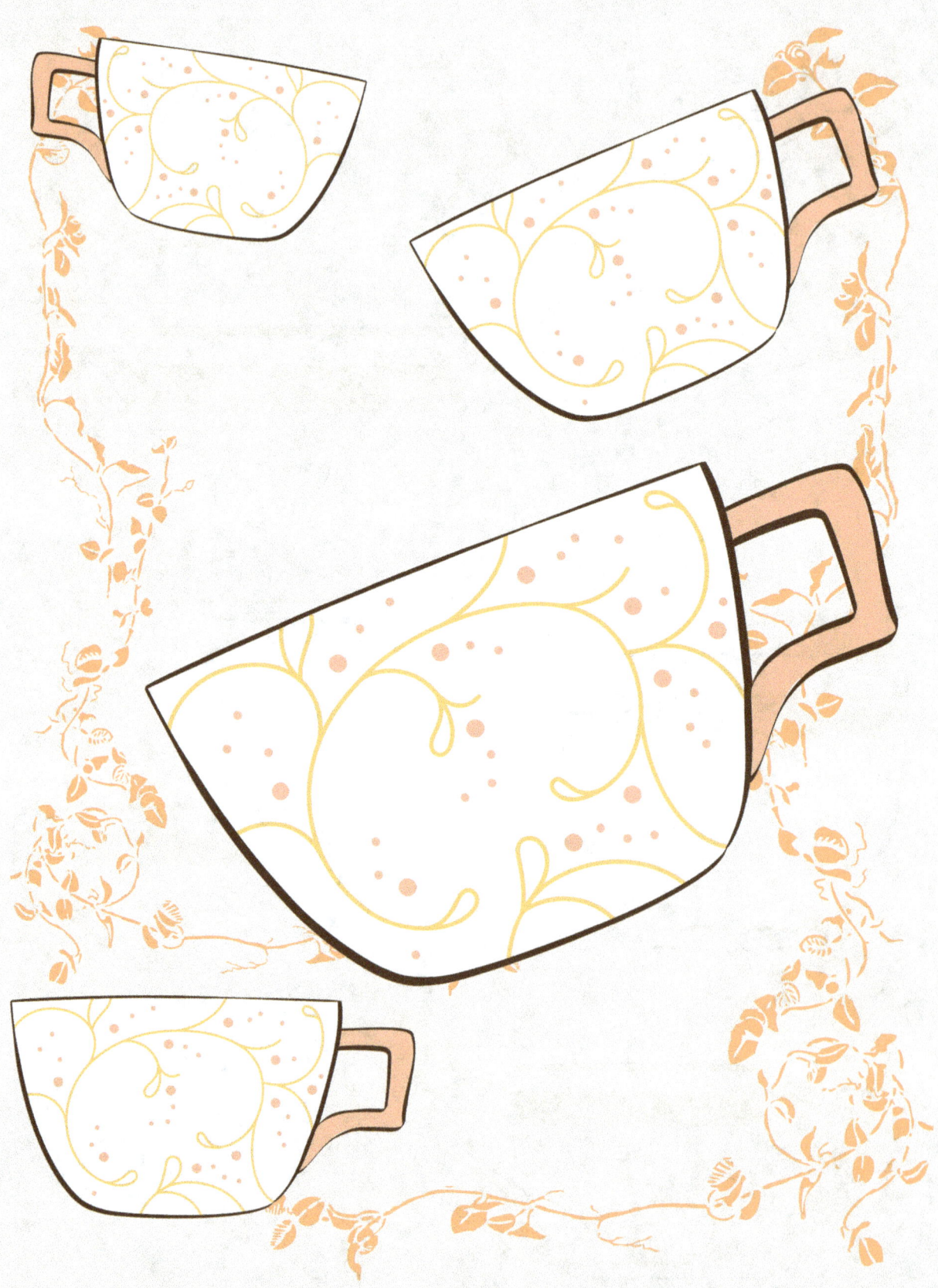

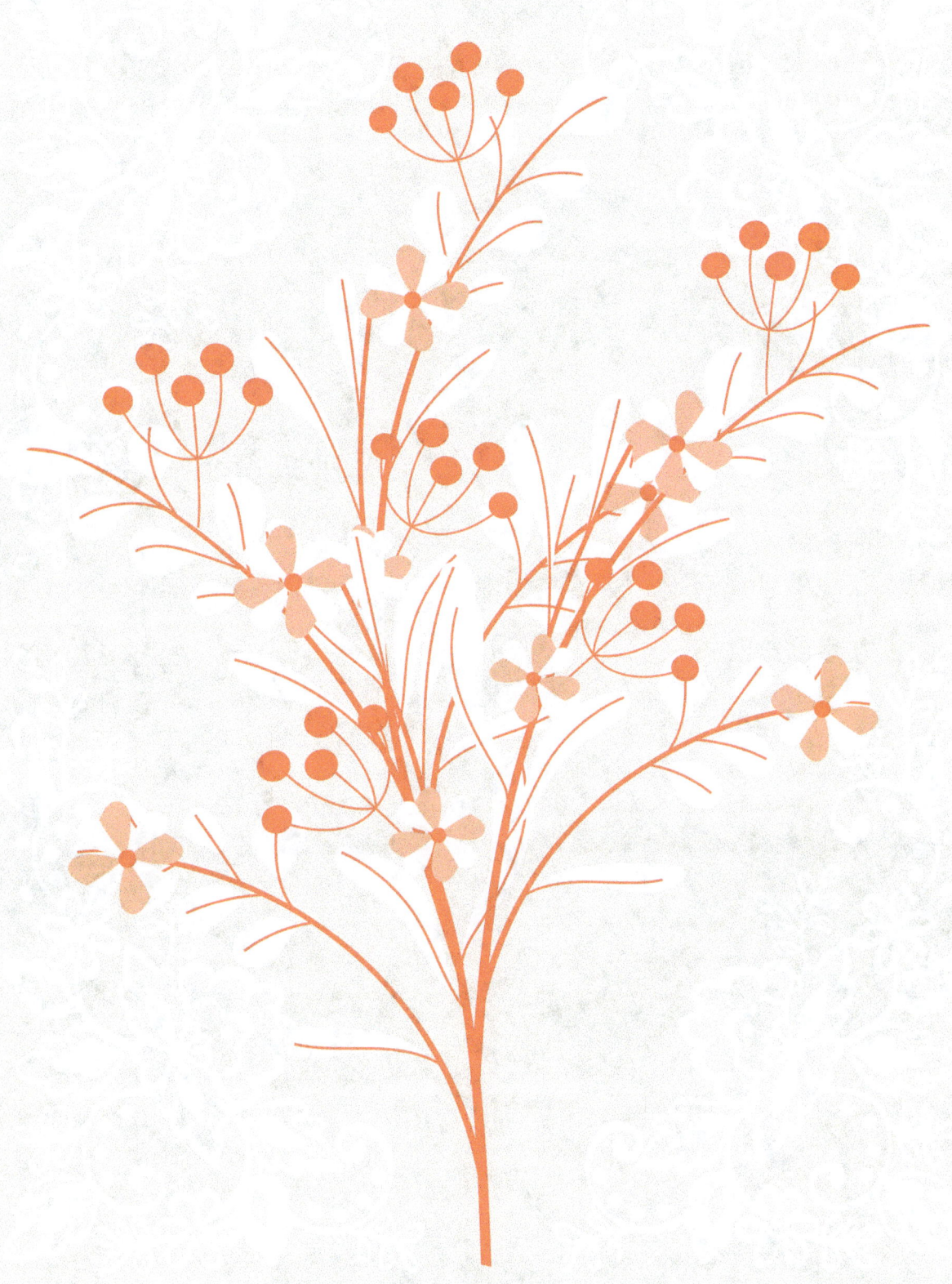

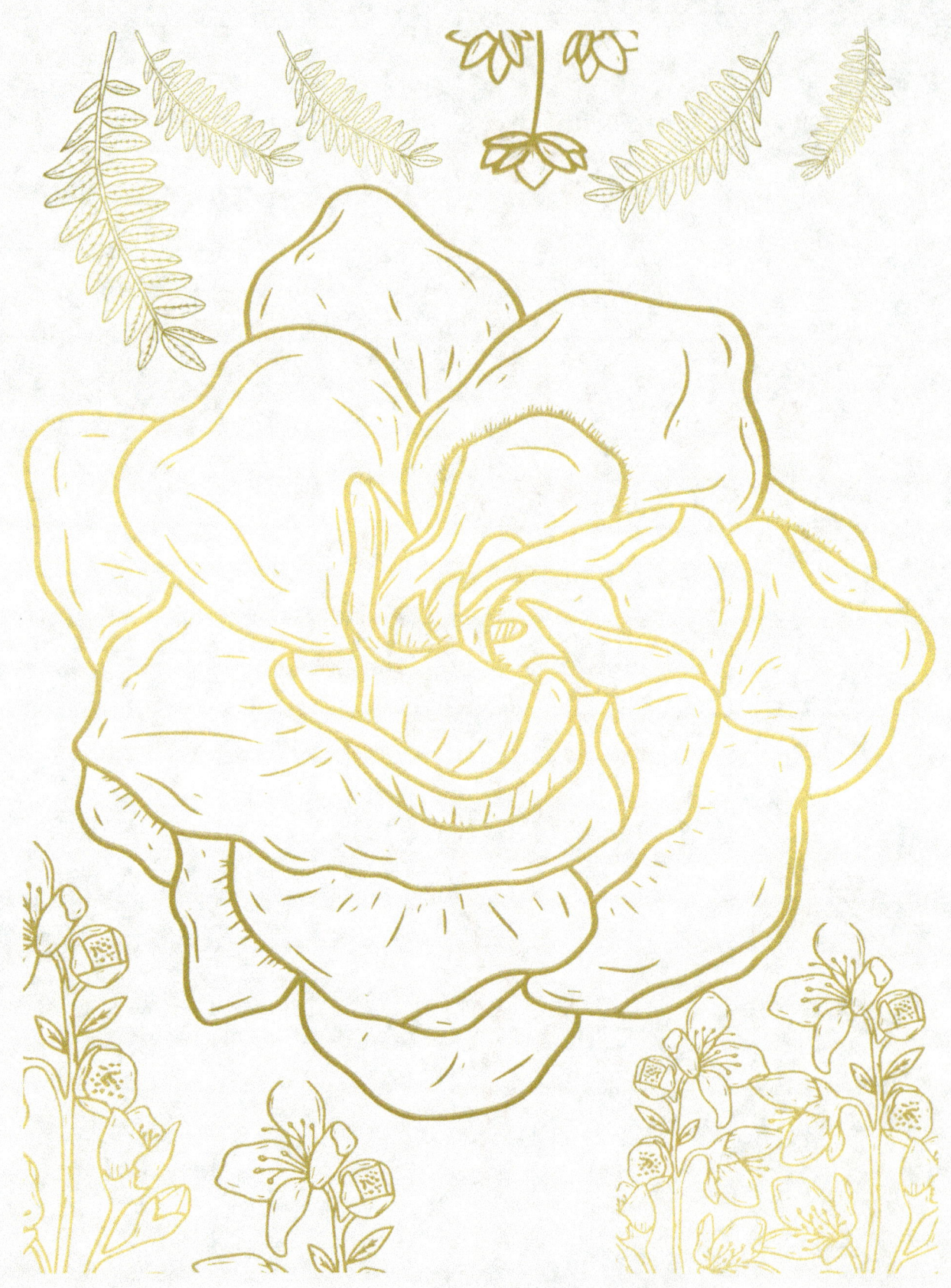

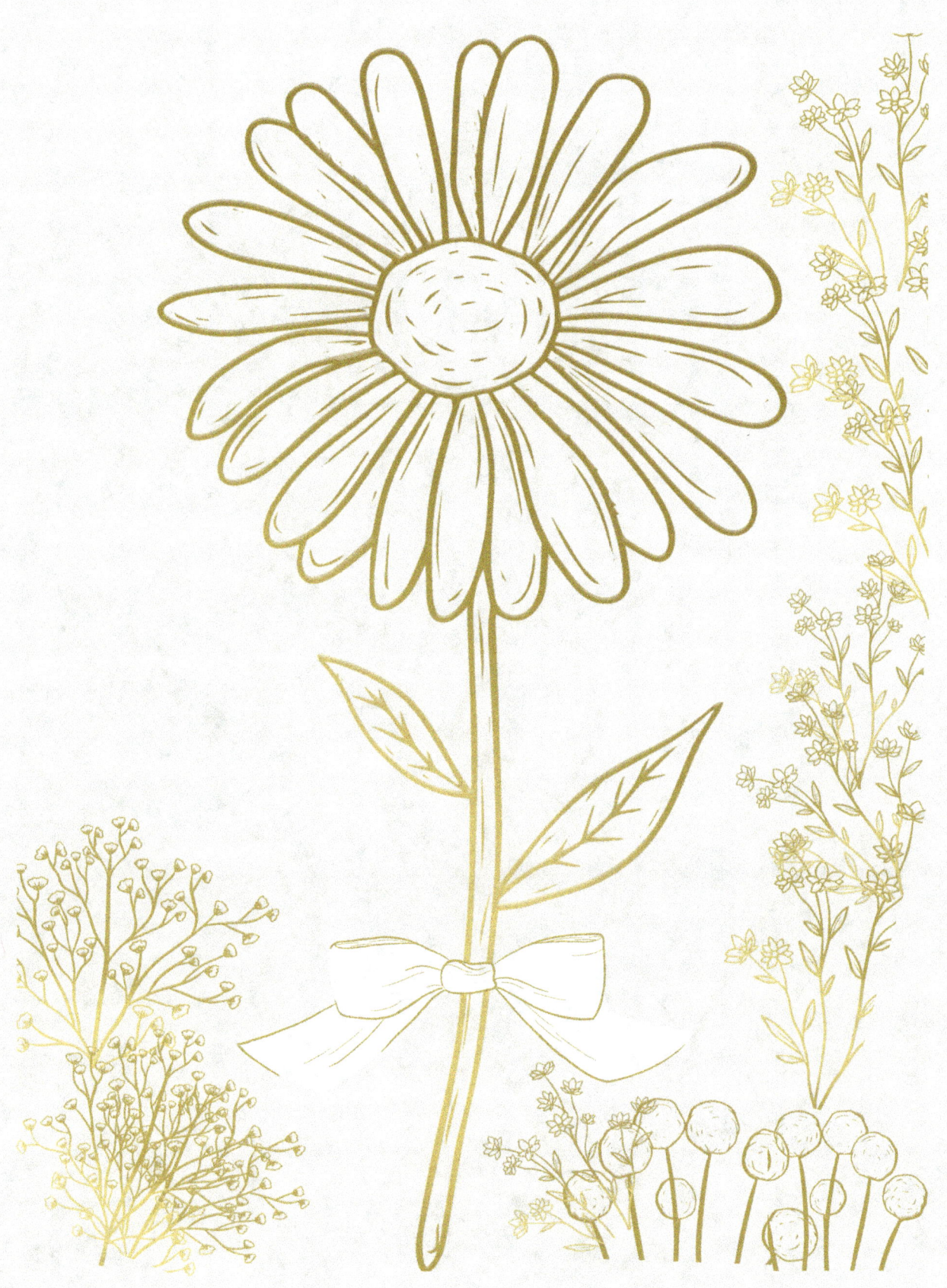

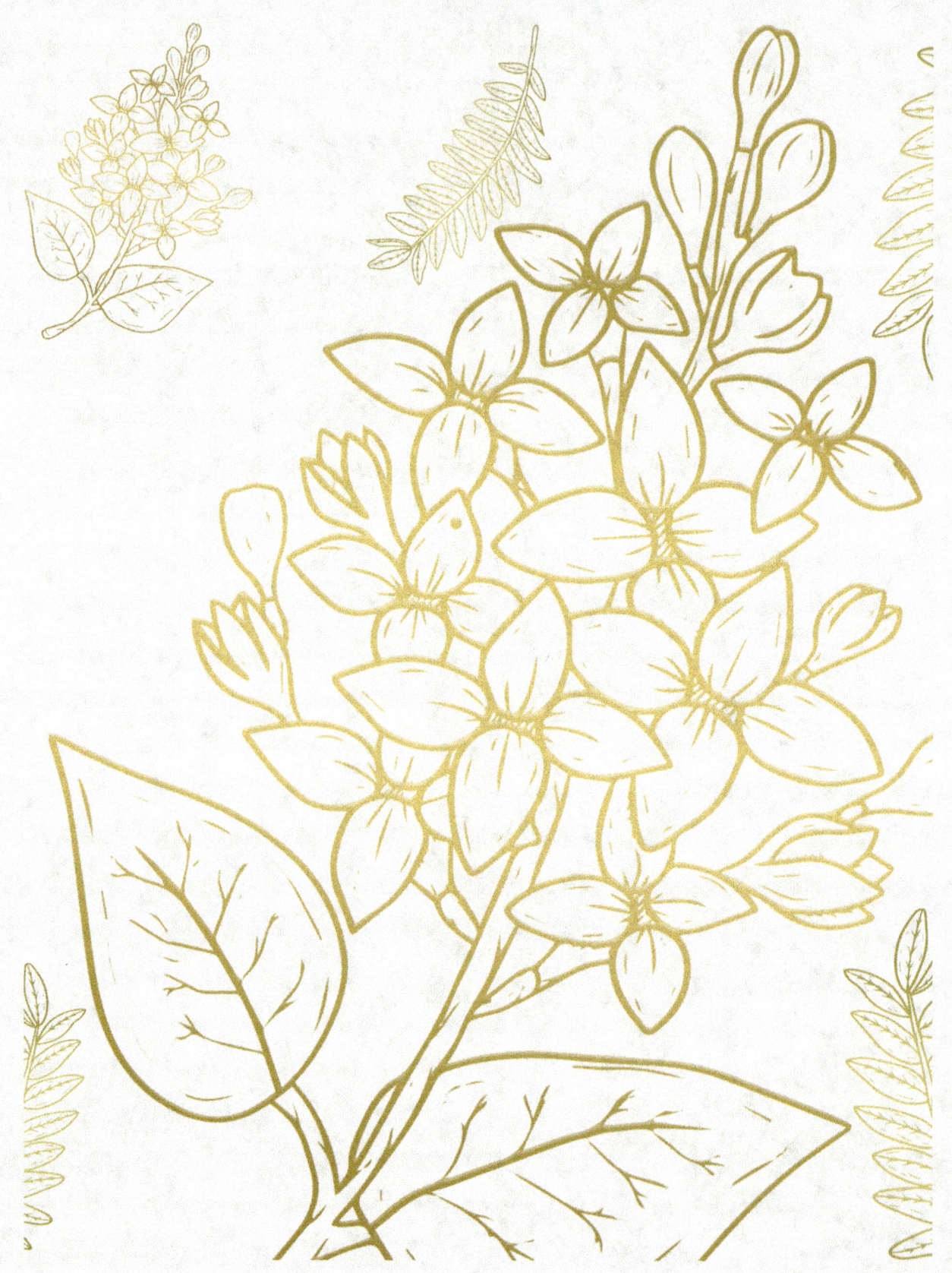

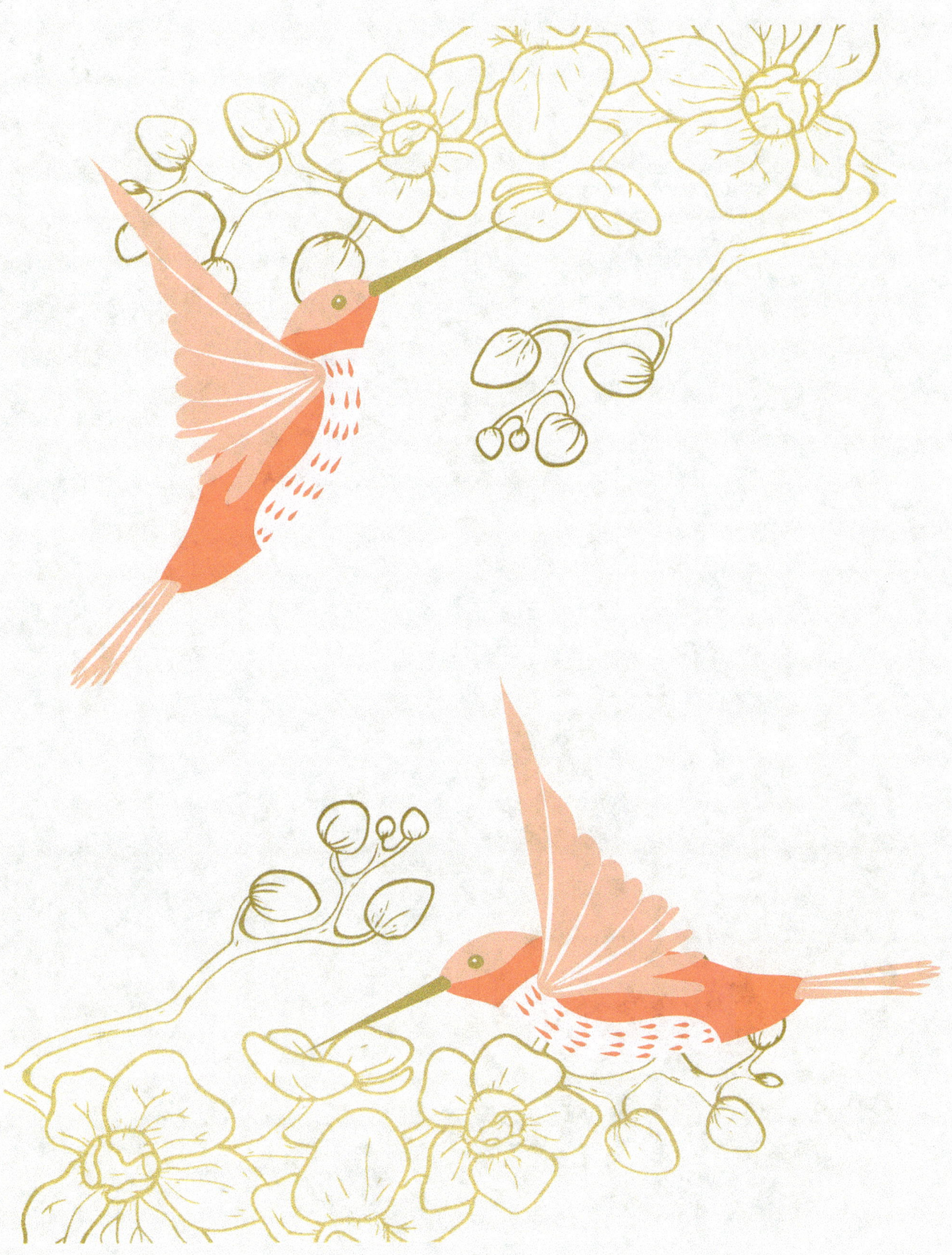

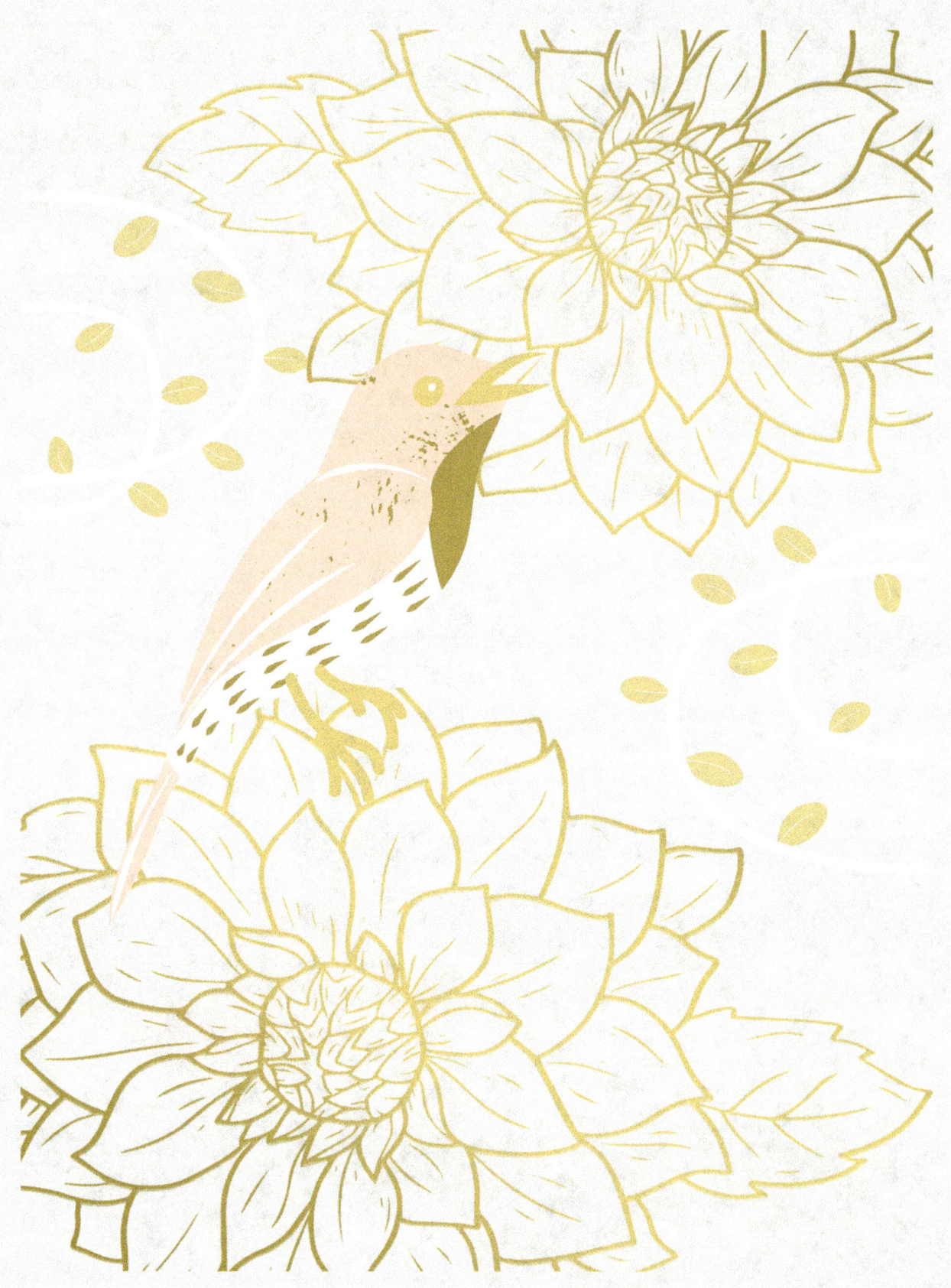

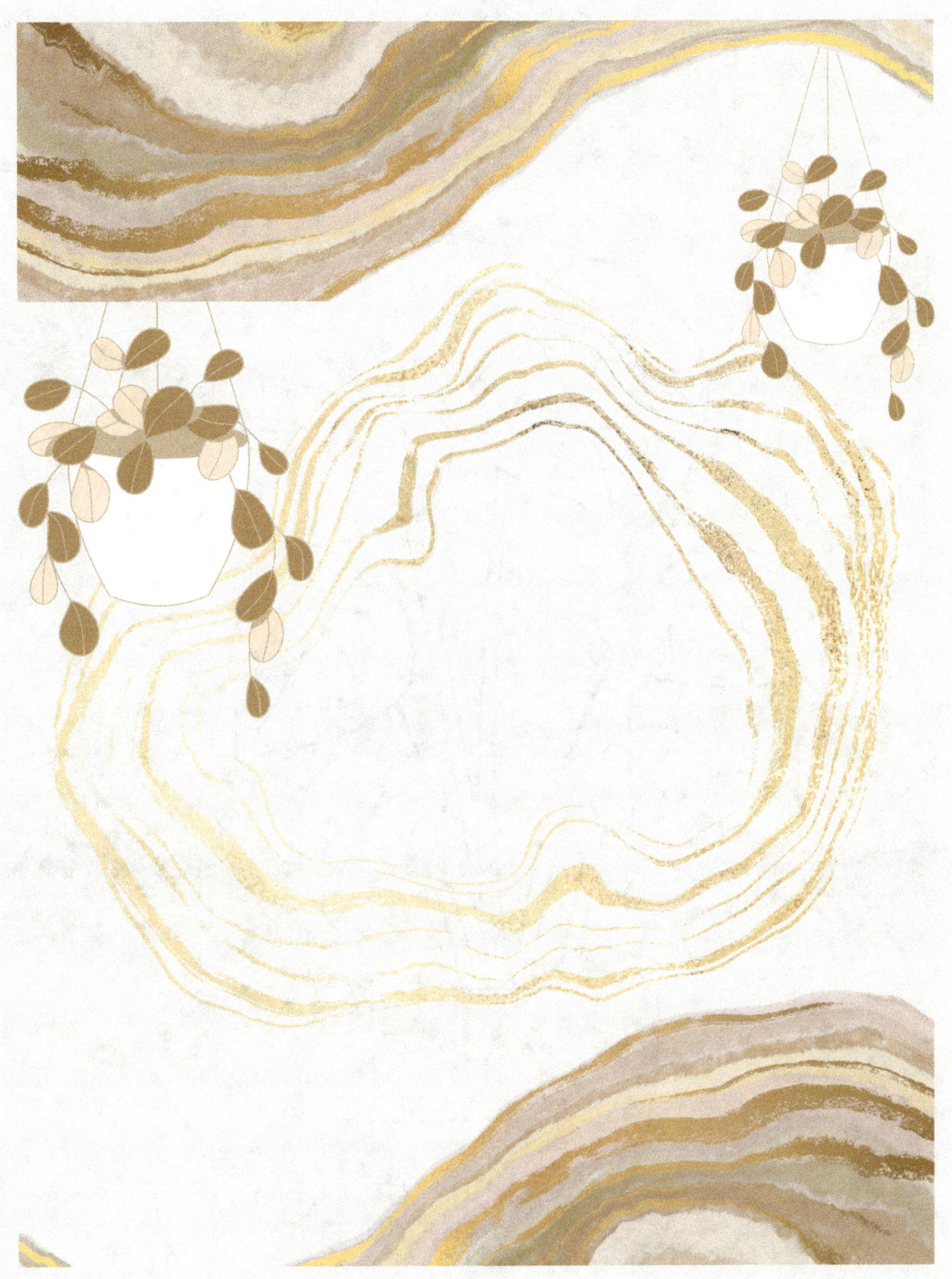

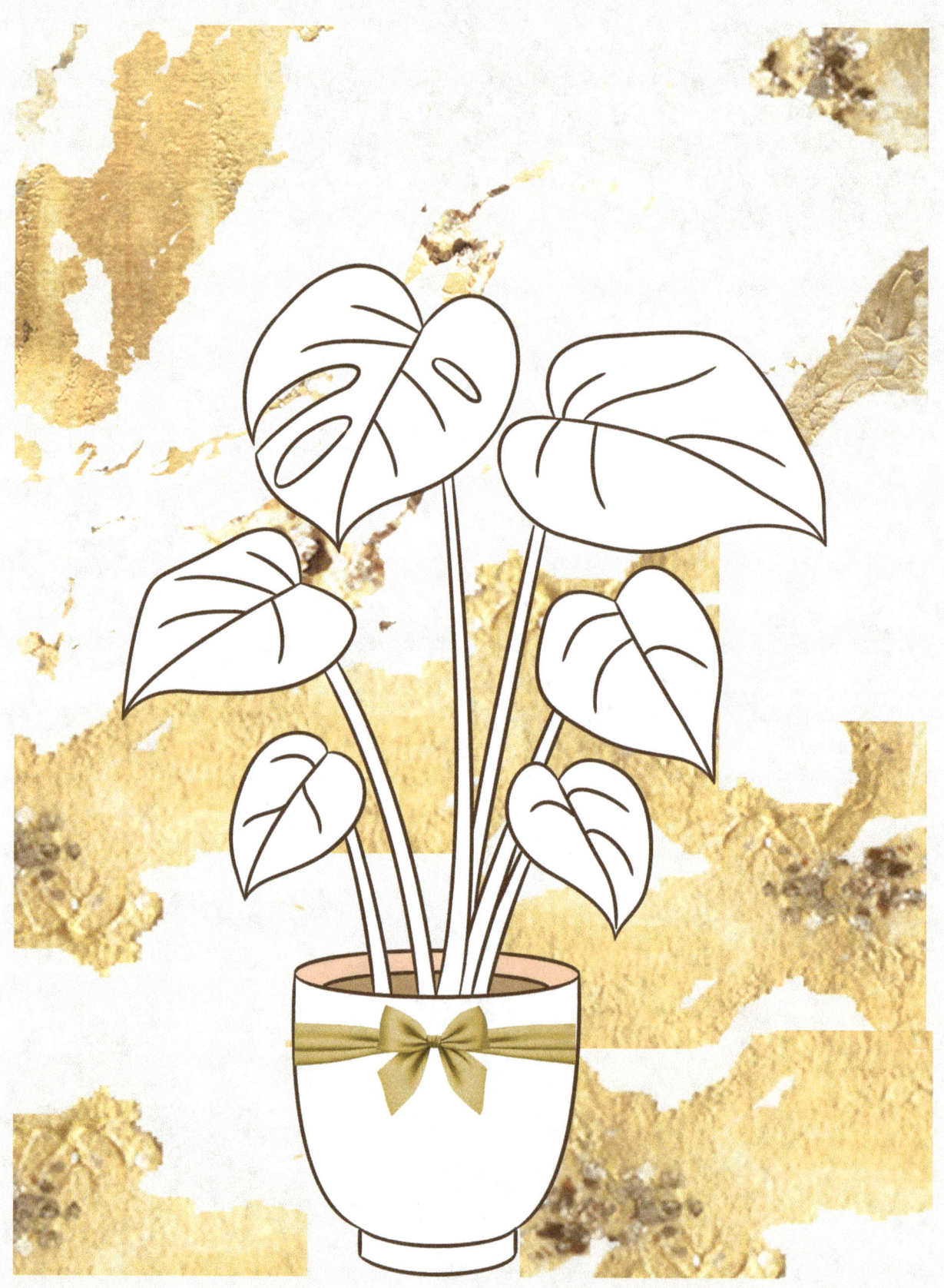

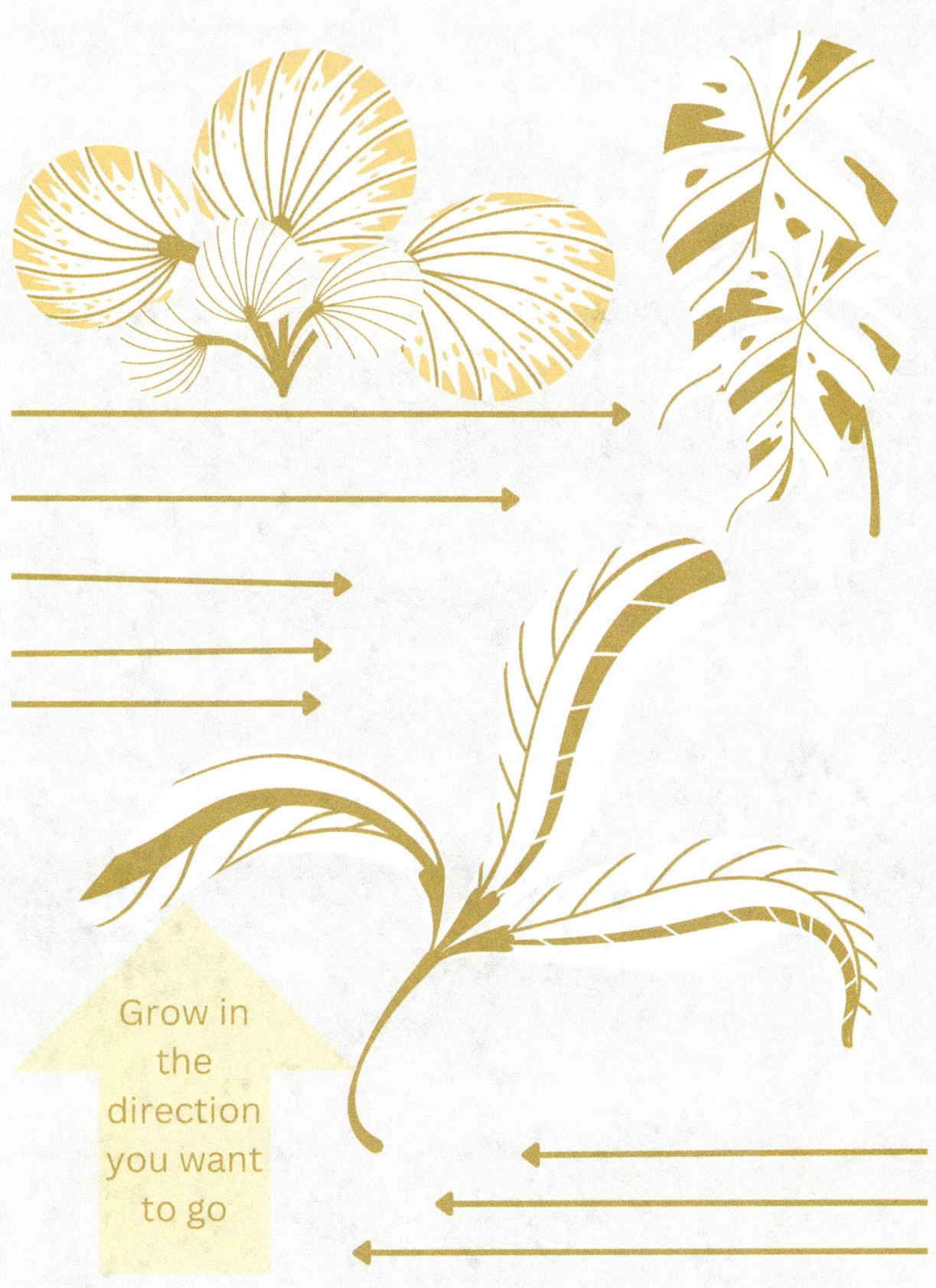

Grow in
the
direction
you want
to go

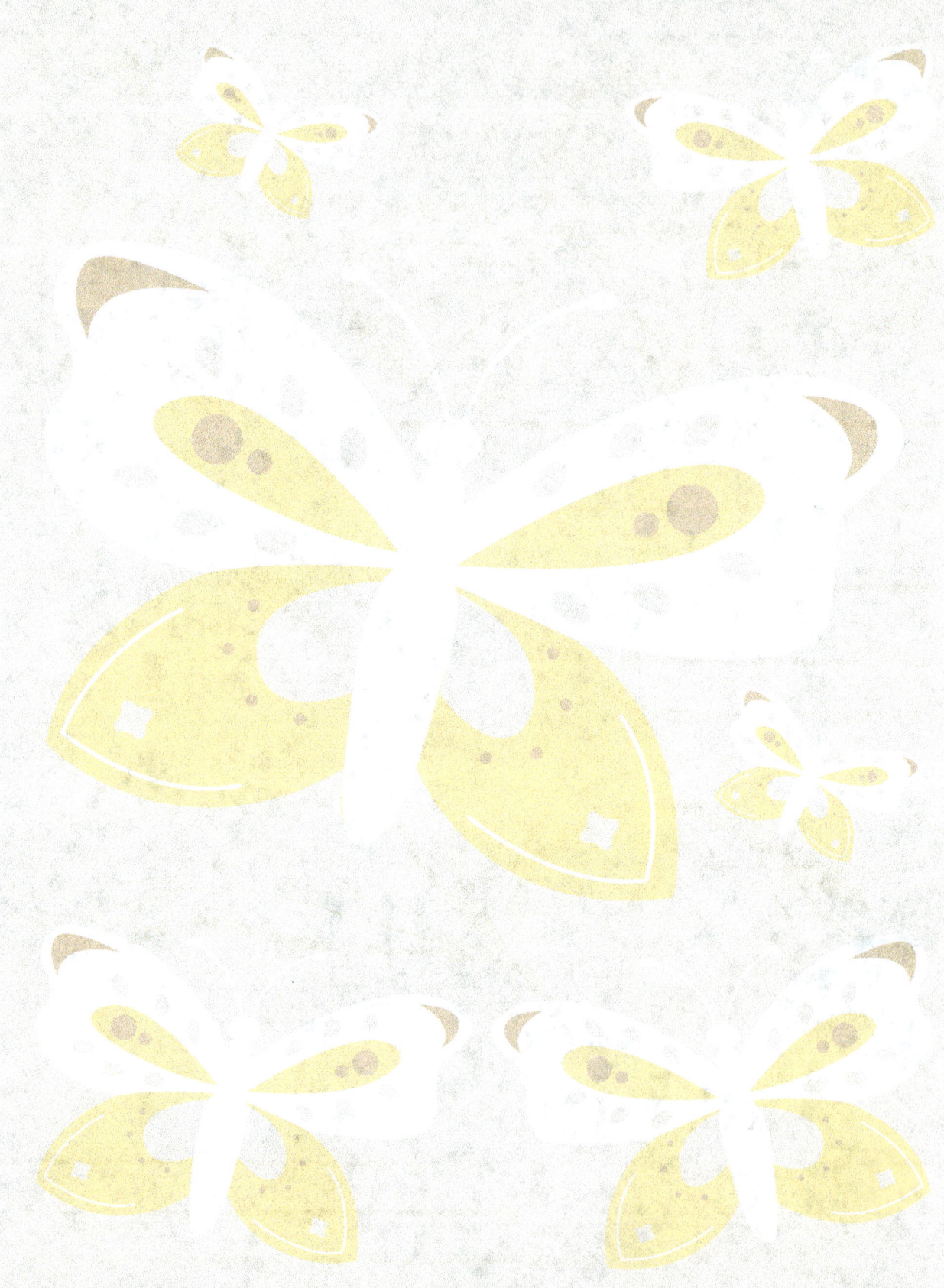

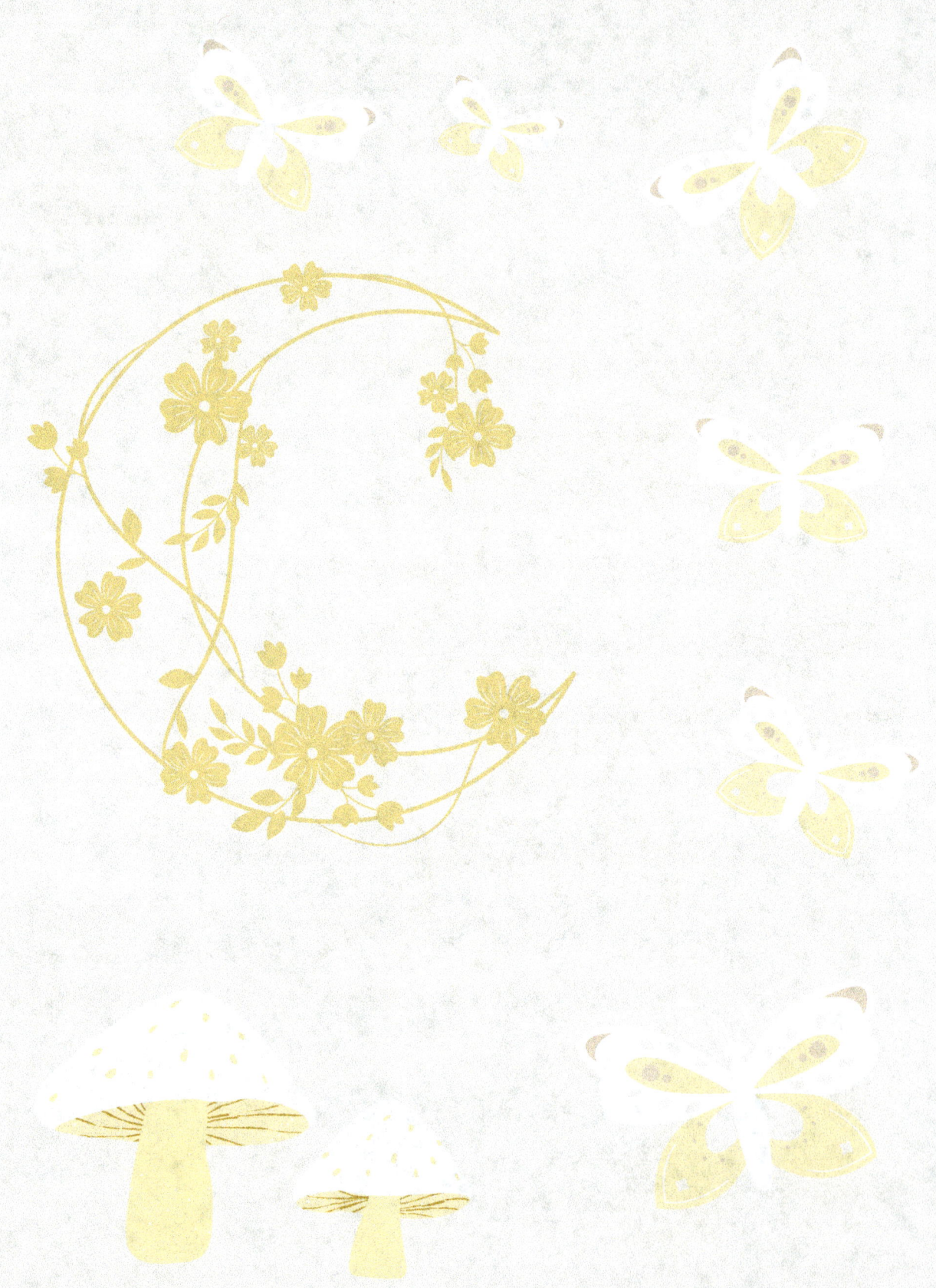

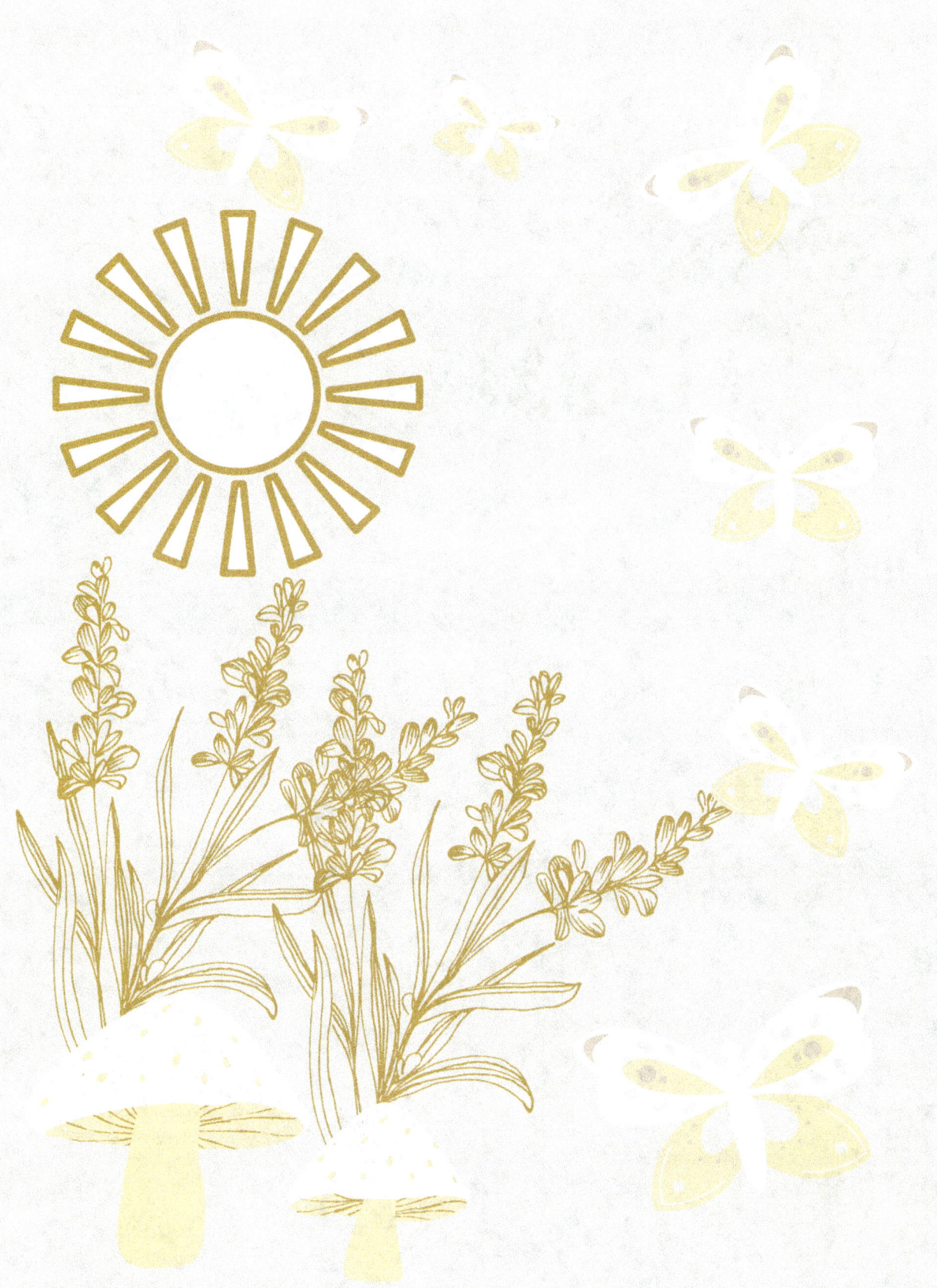

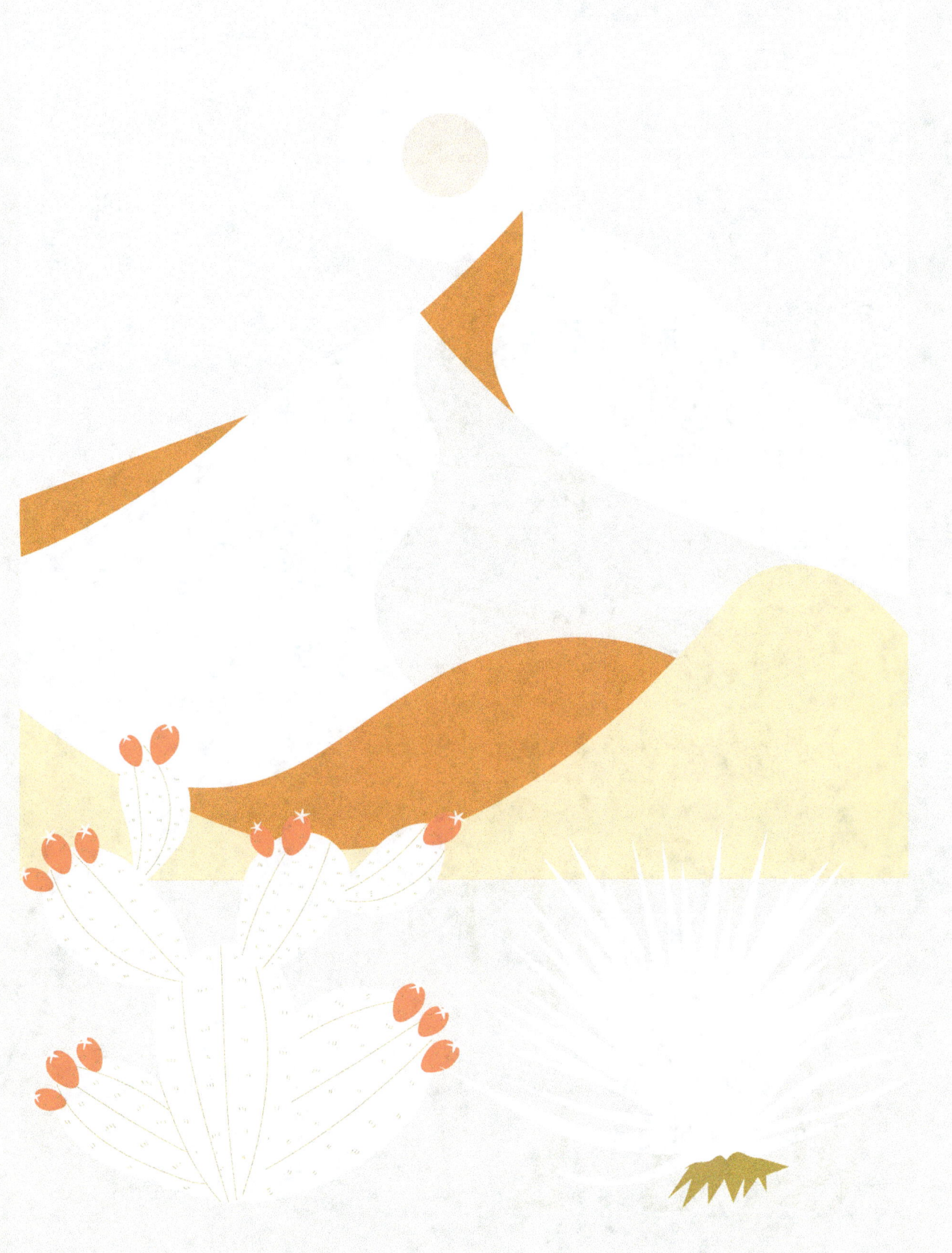

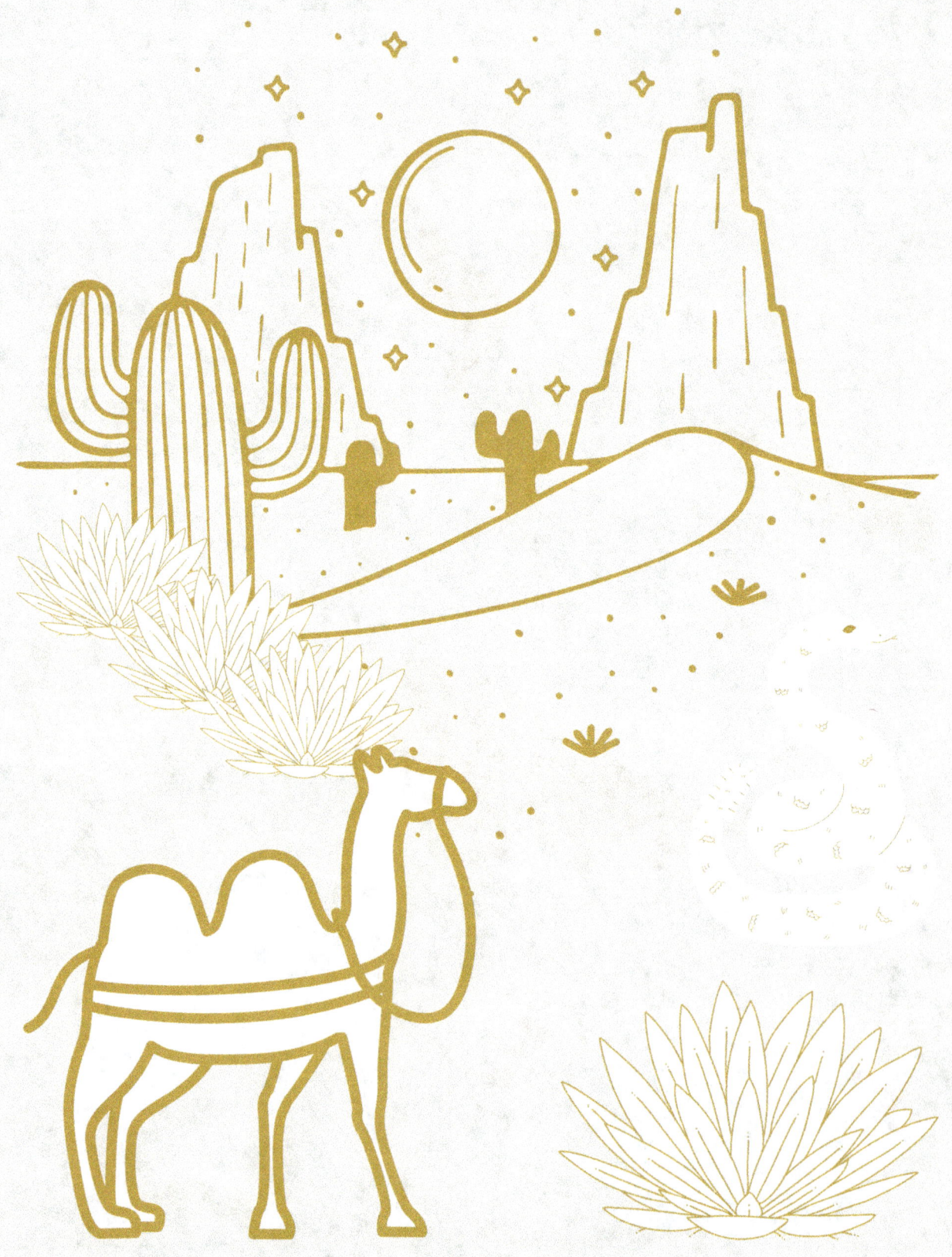

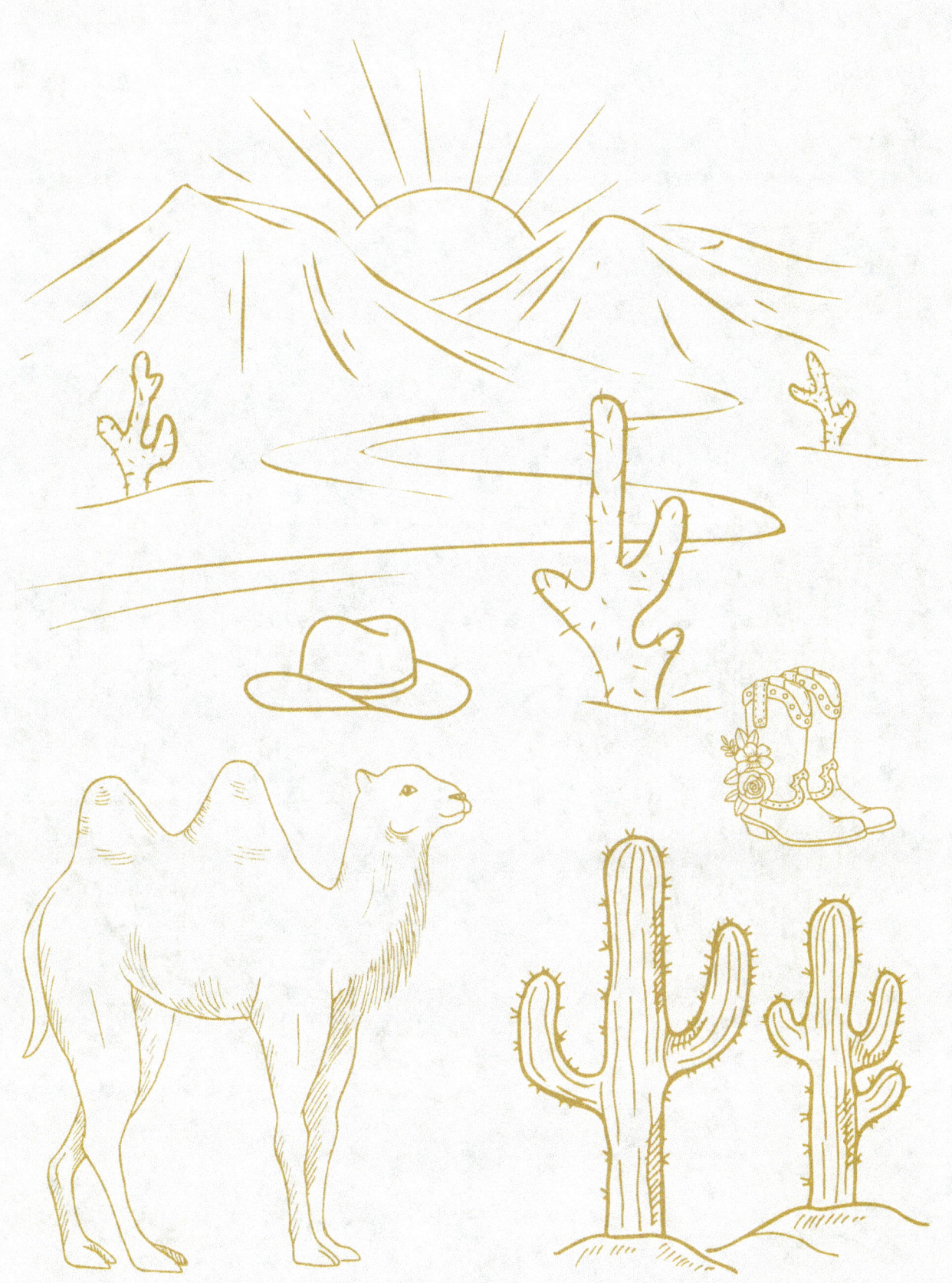

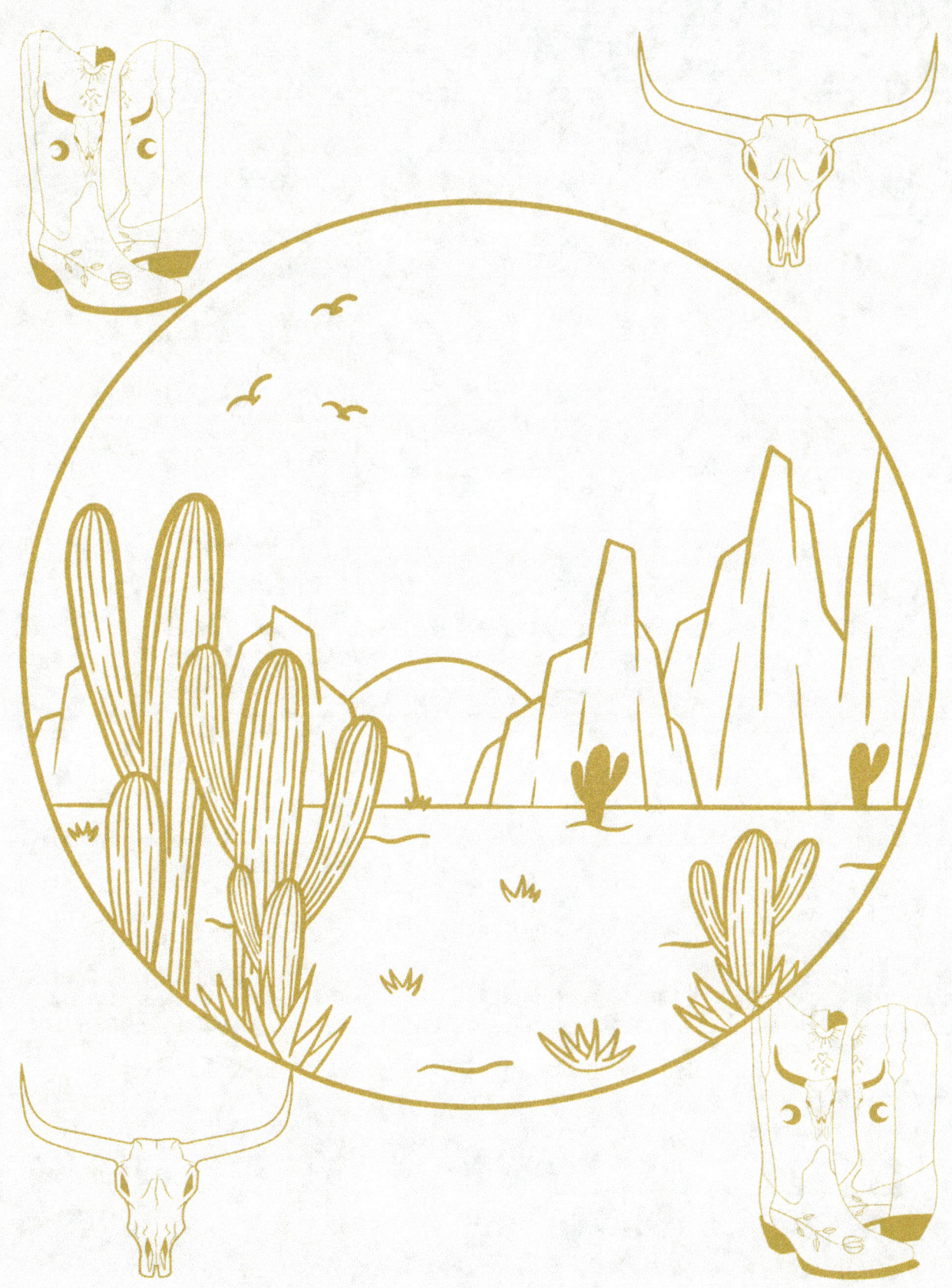

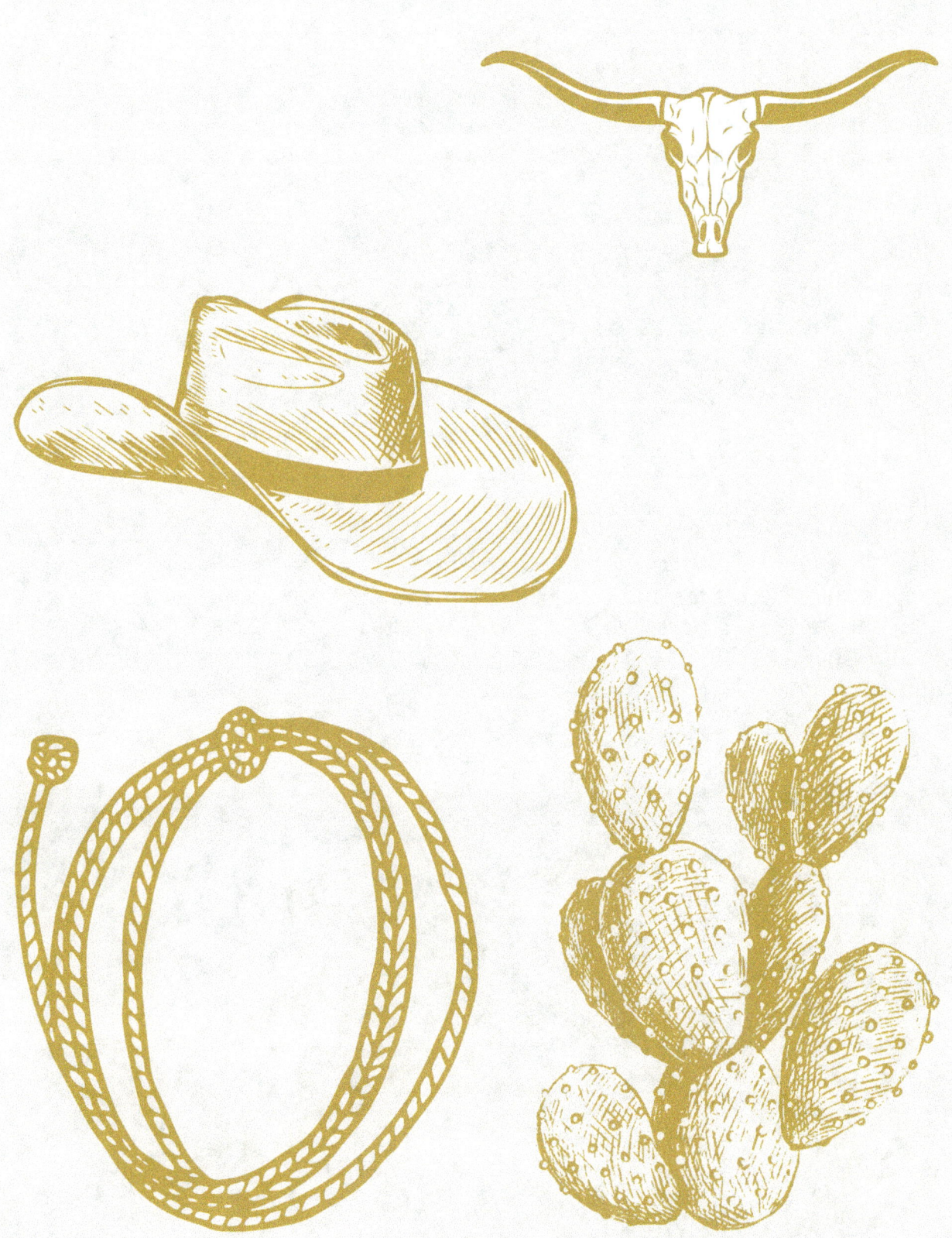

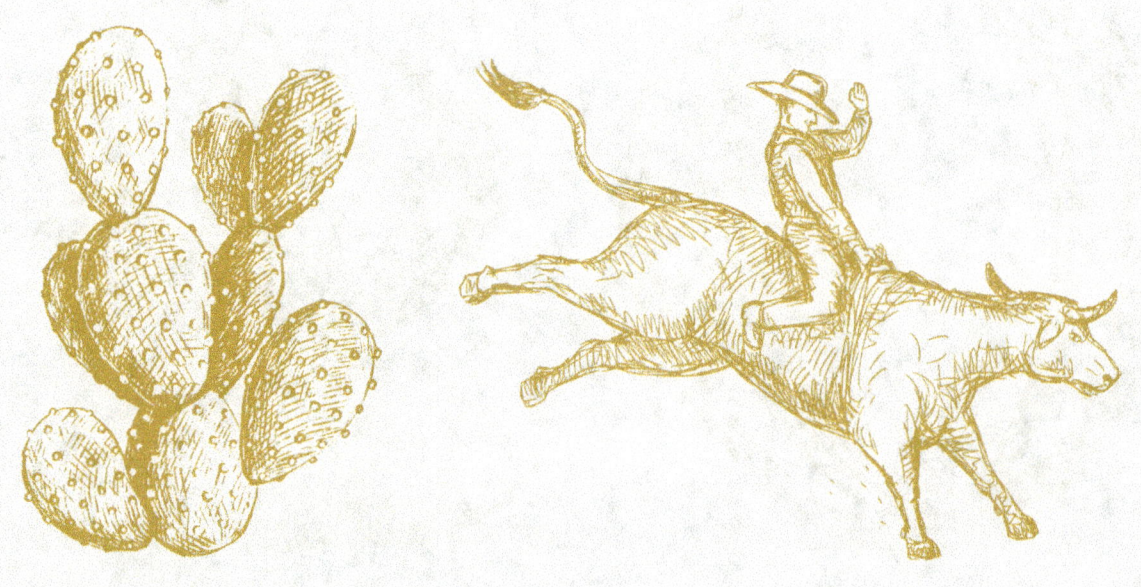

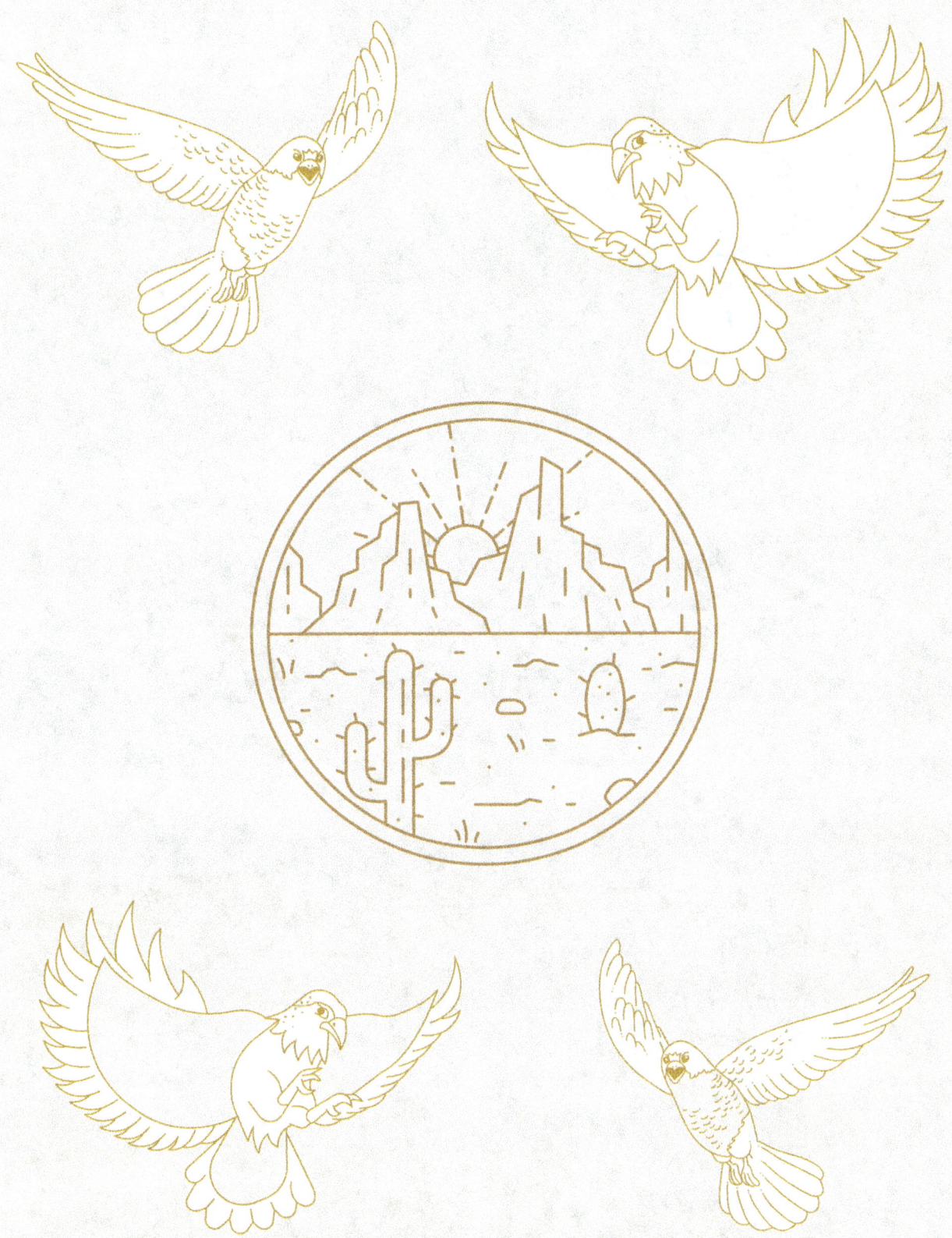

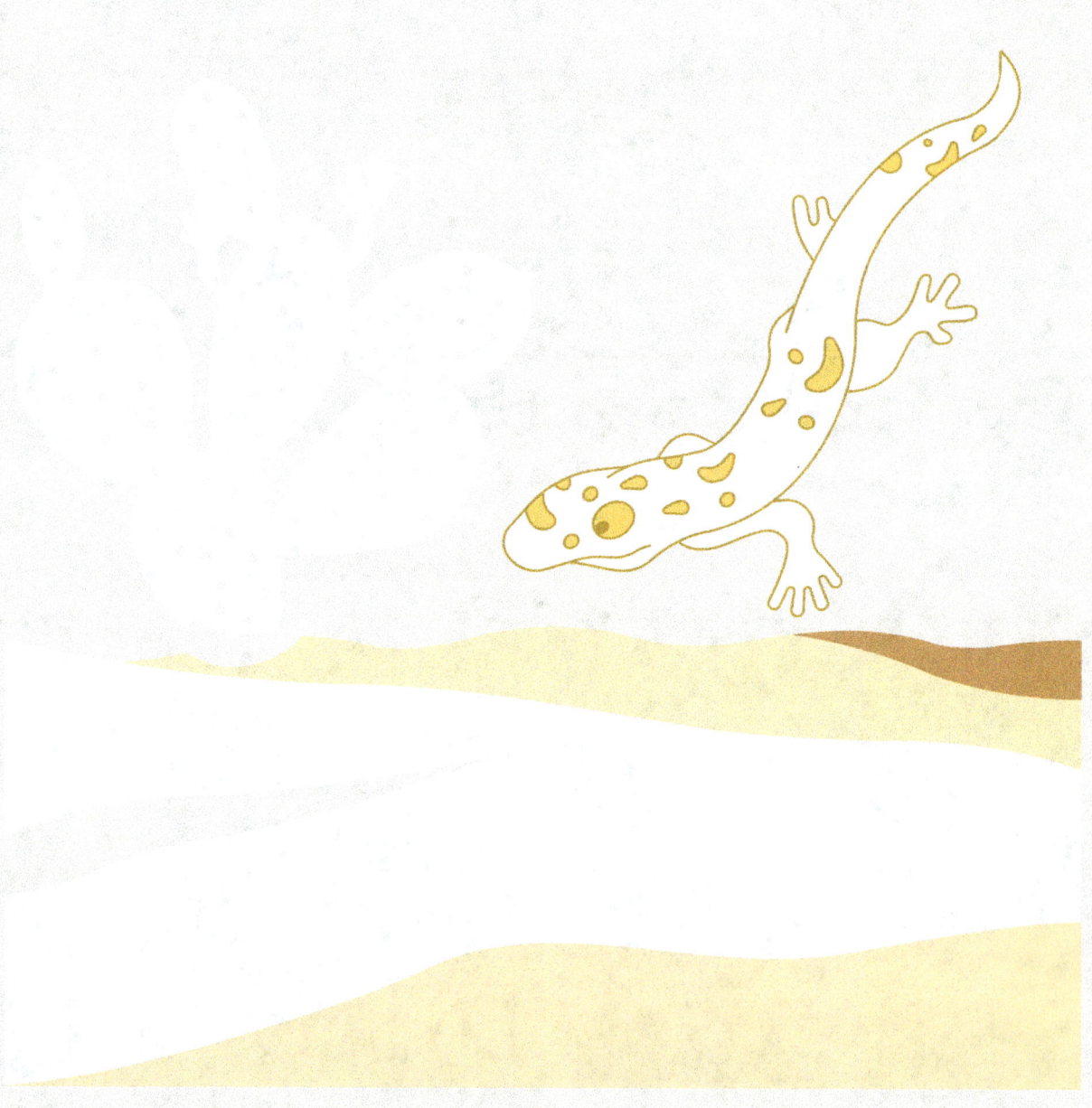

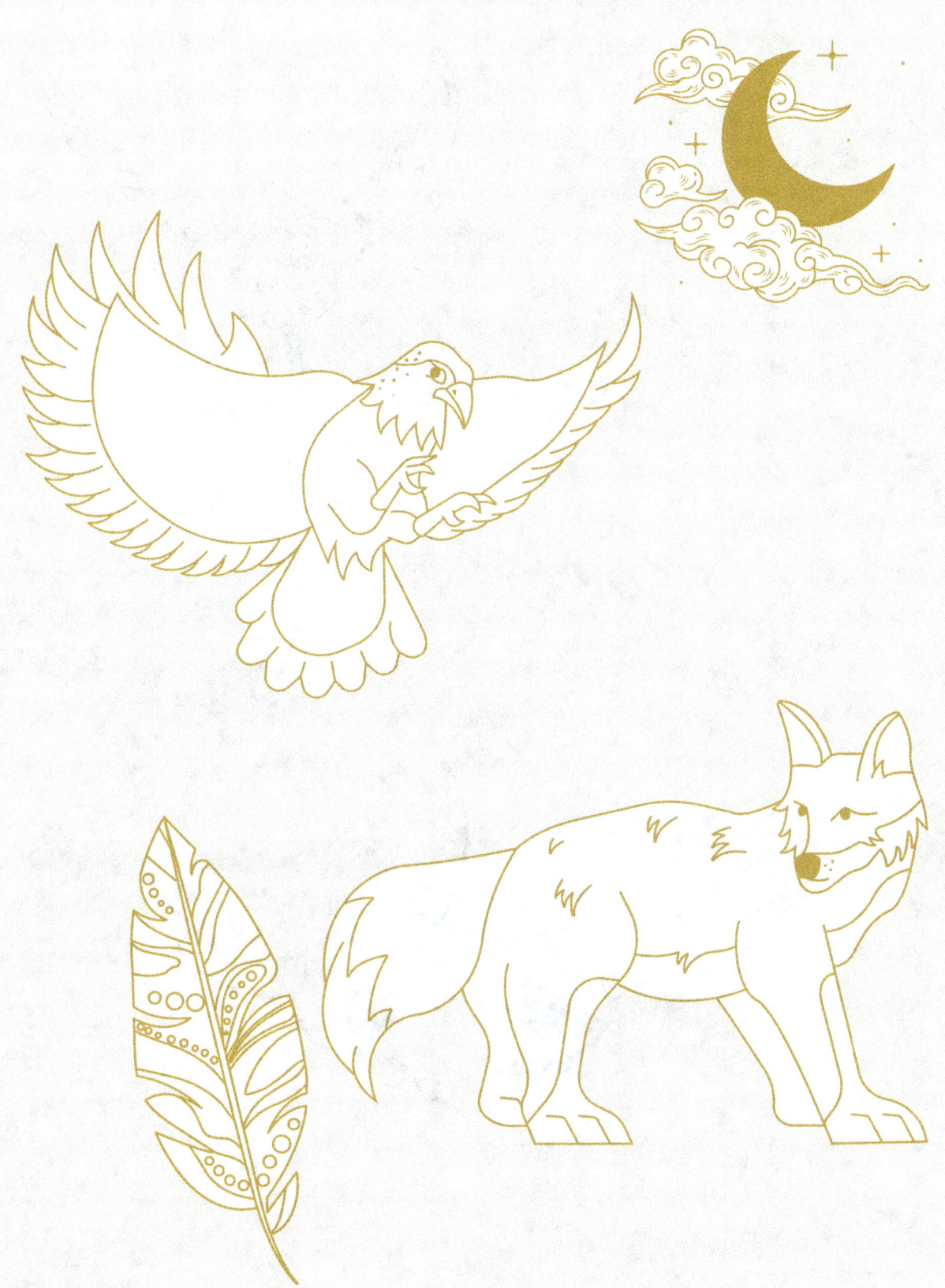

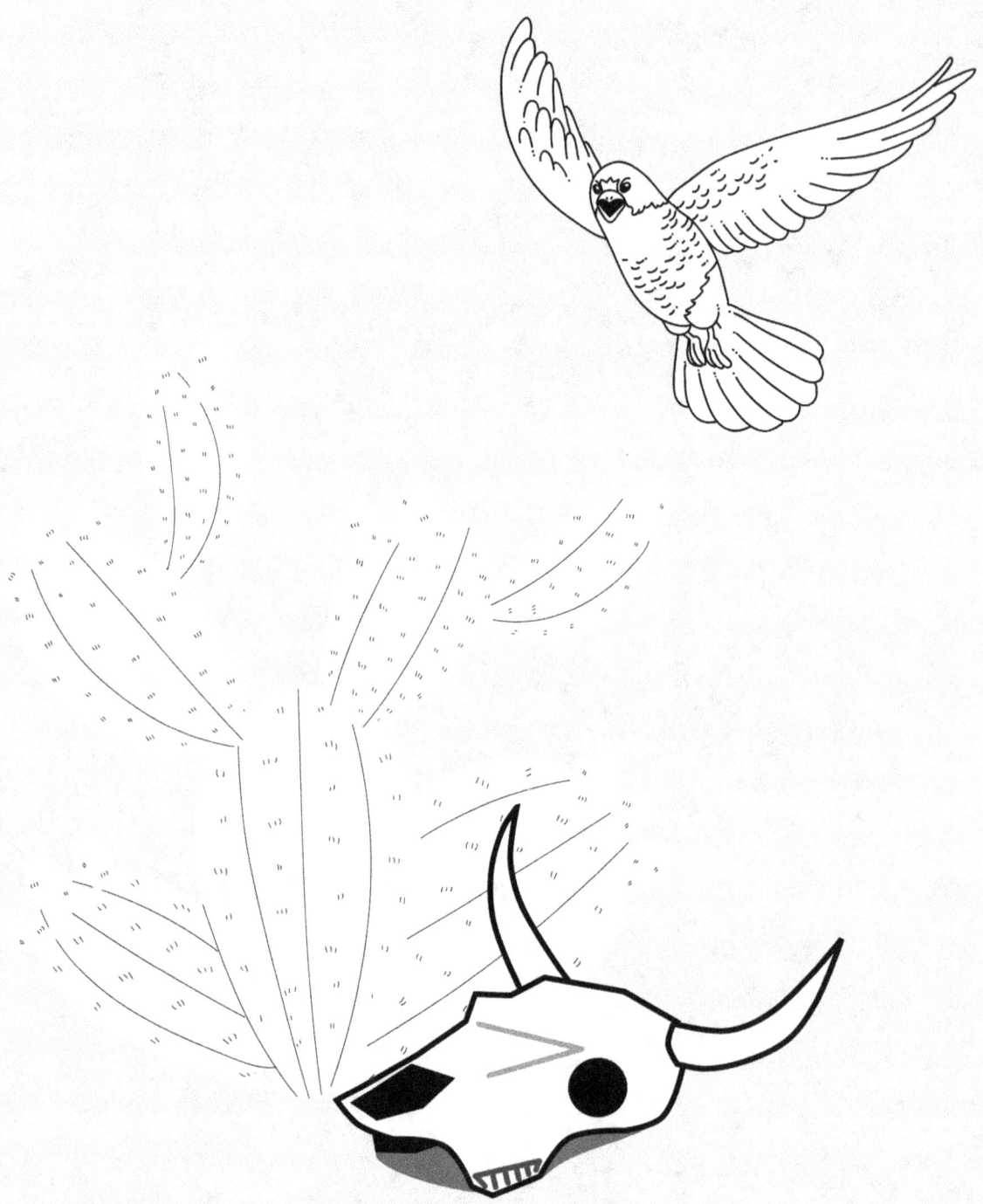

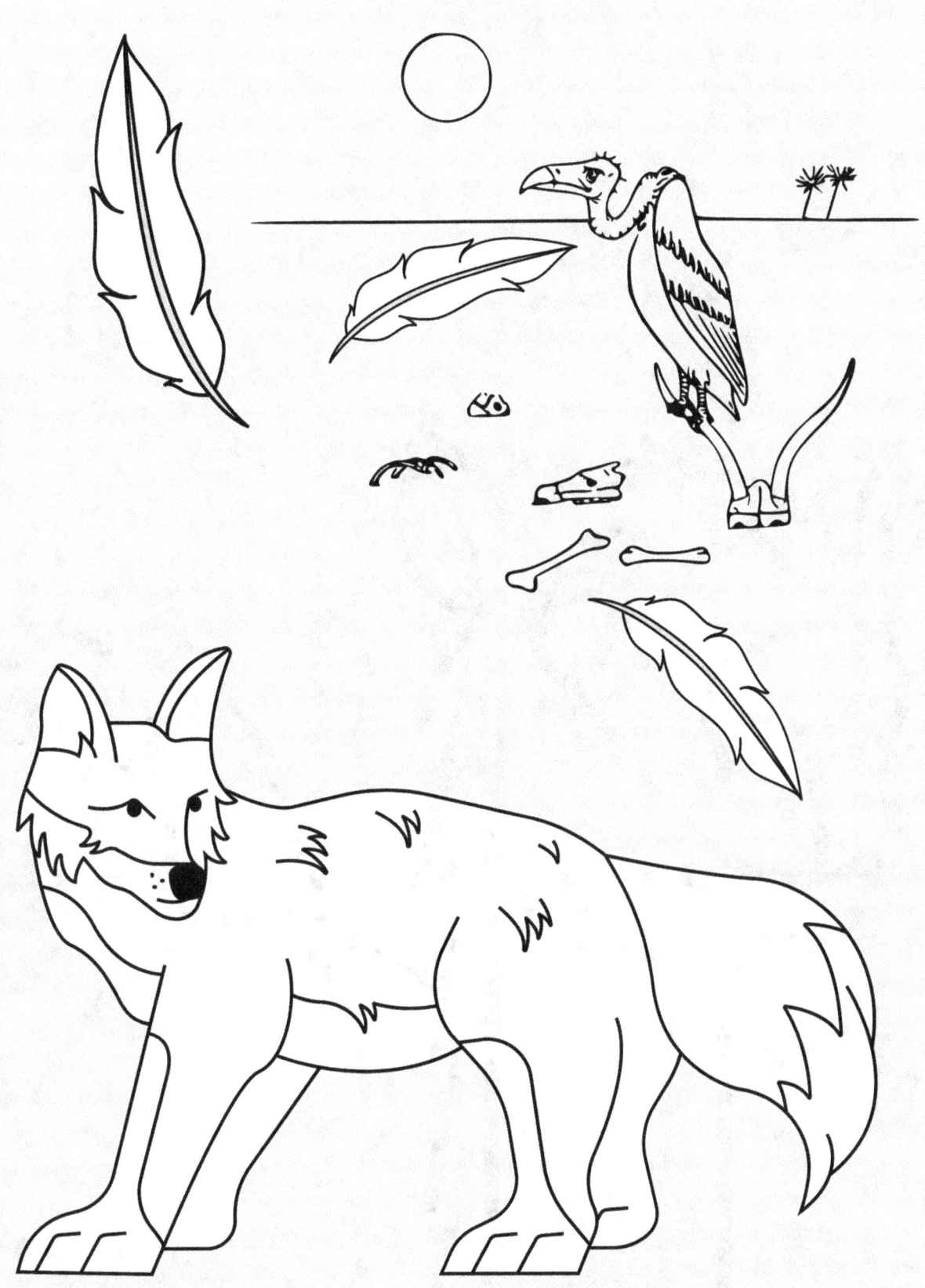

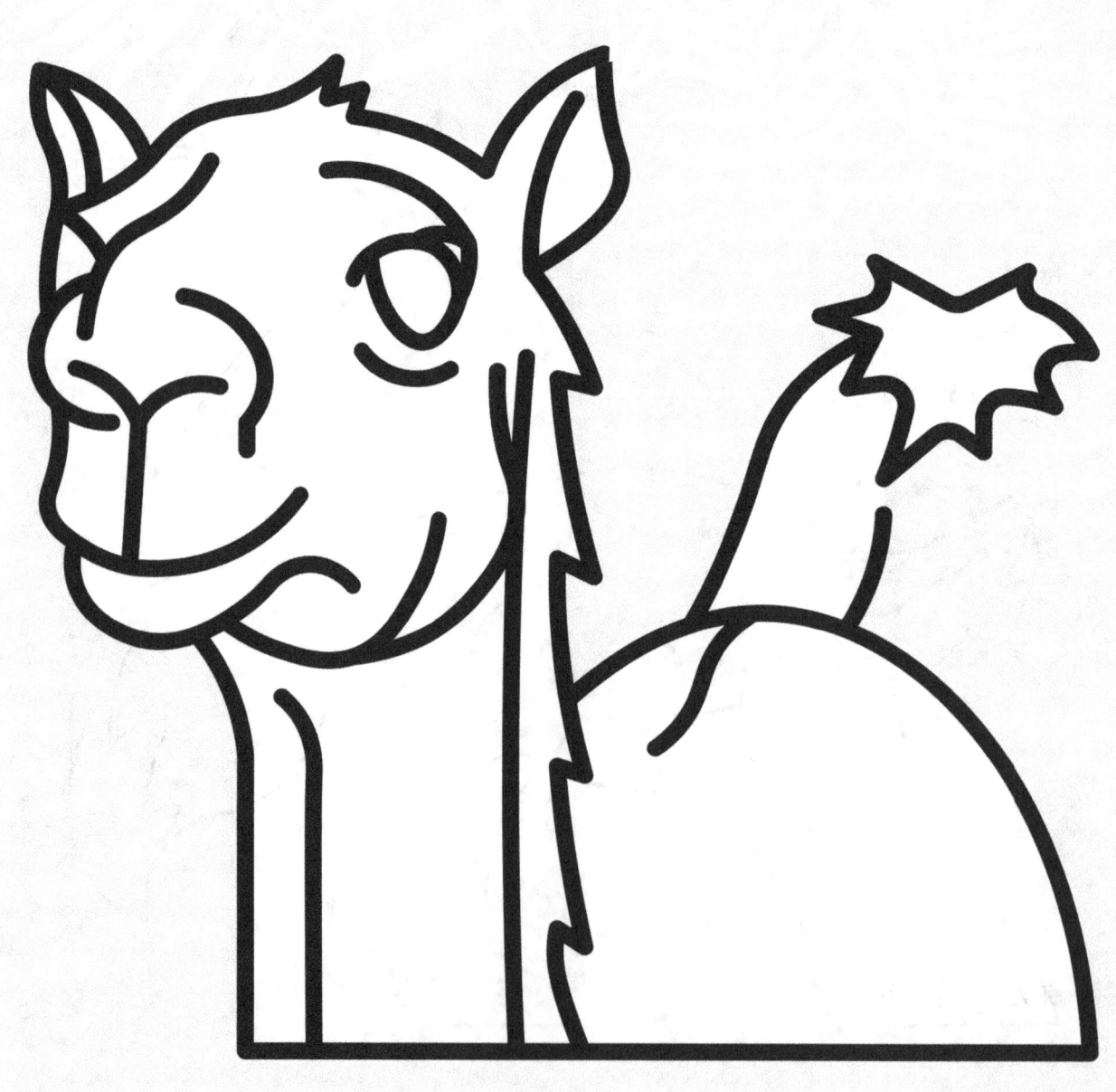

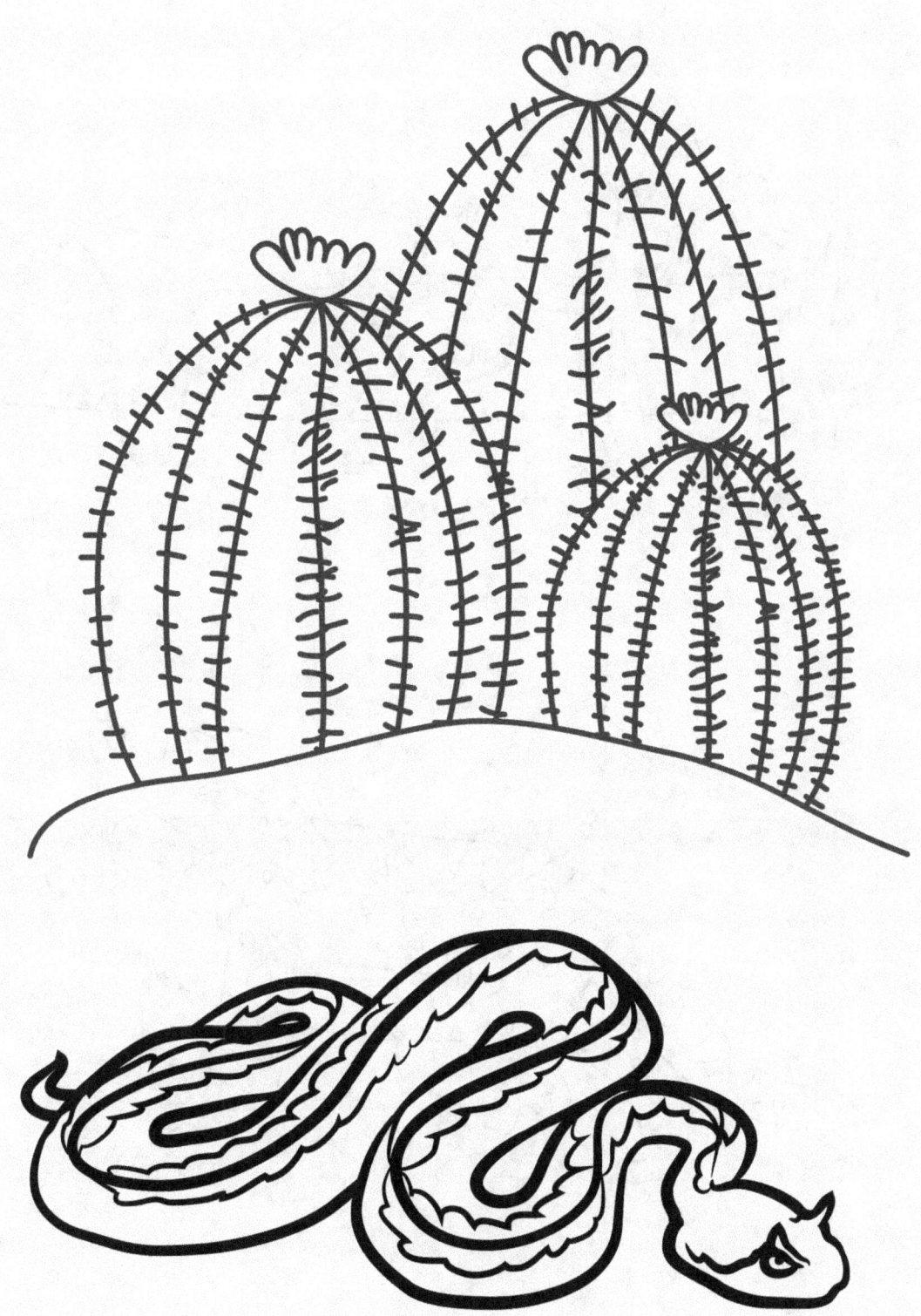

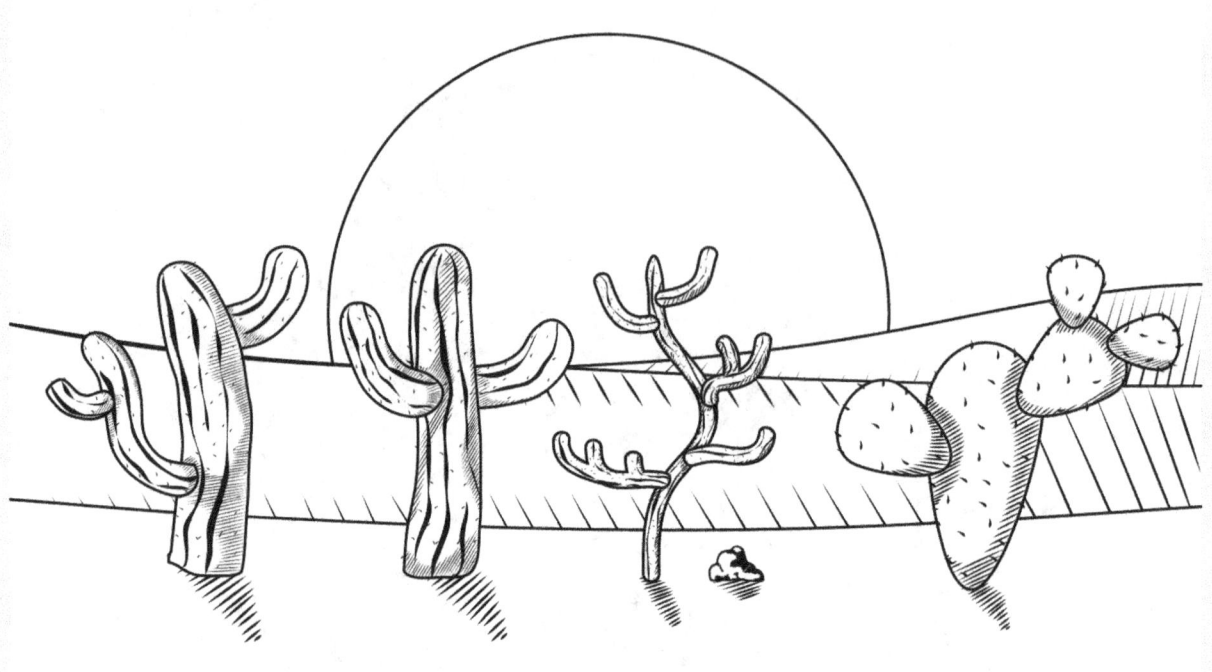

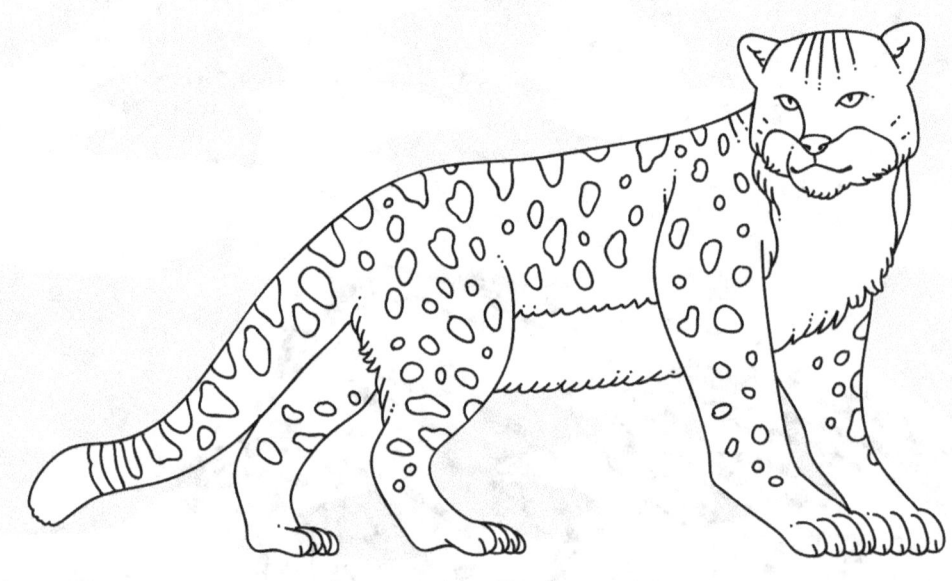

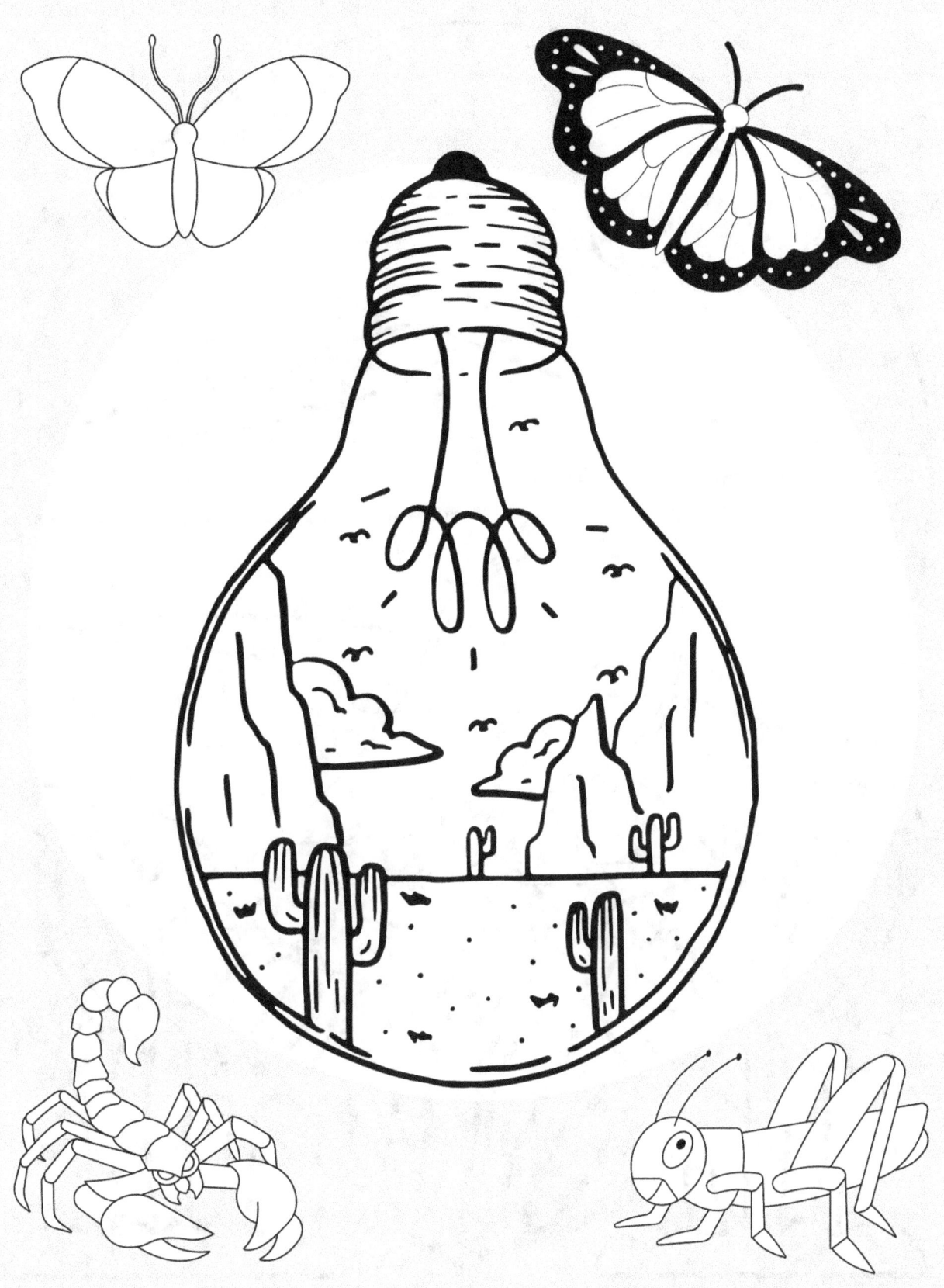

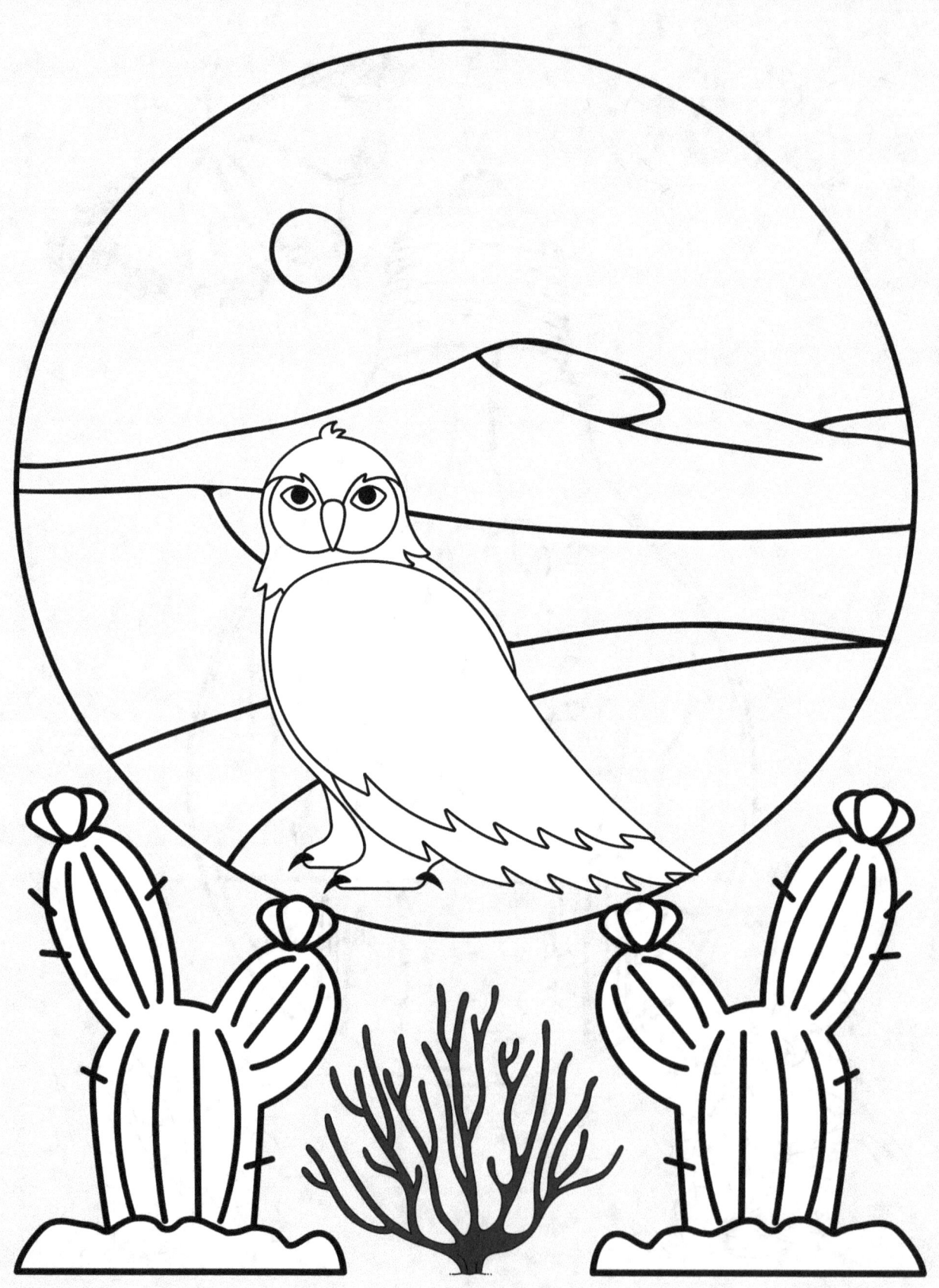

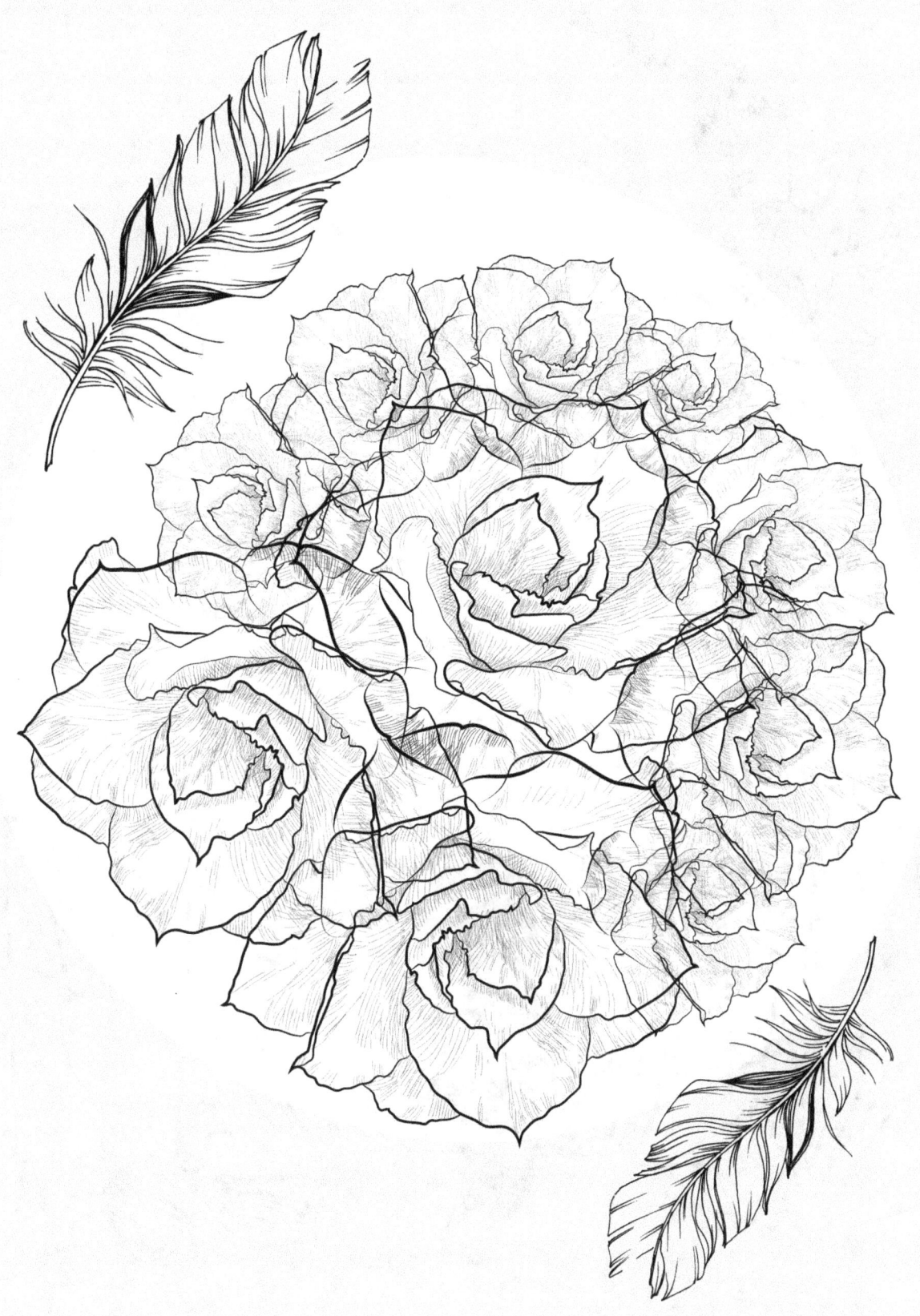

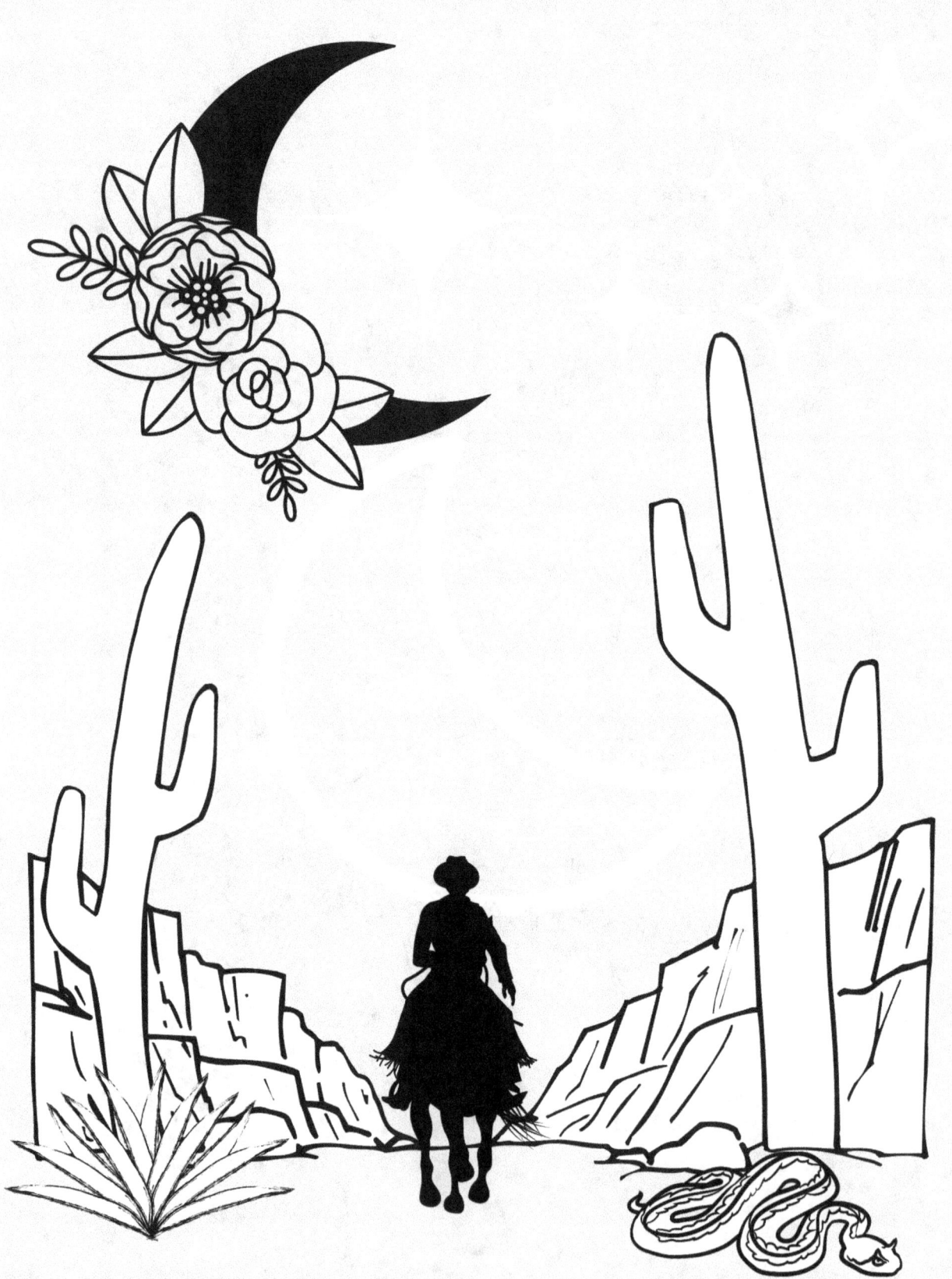

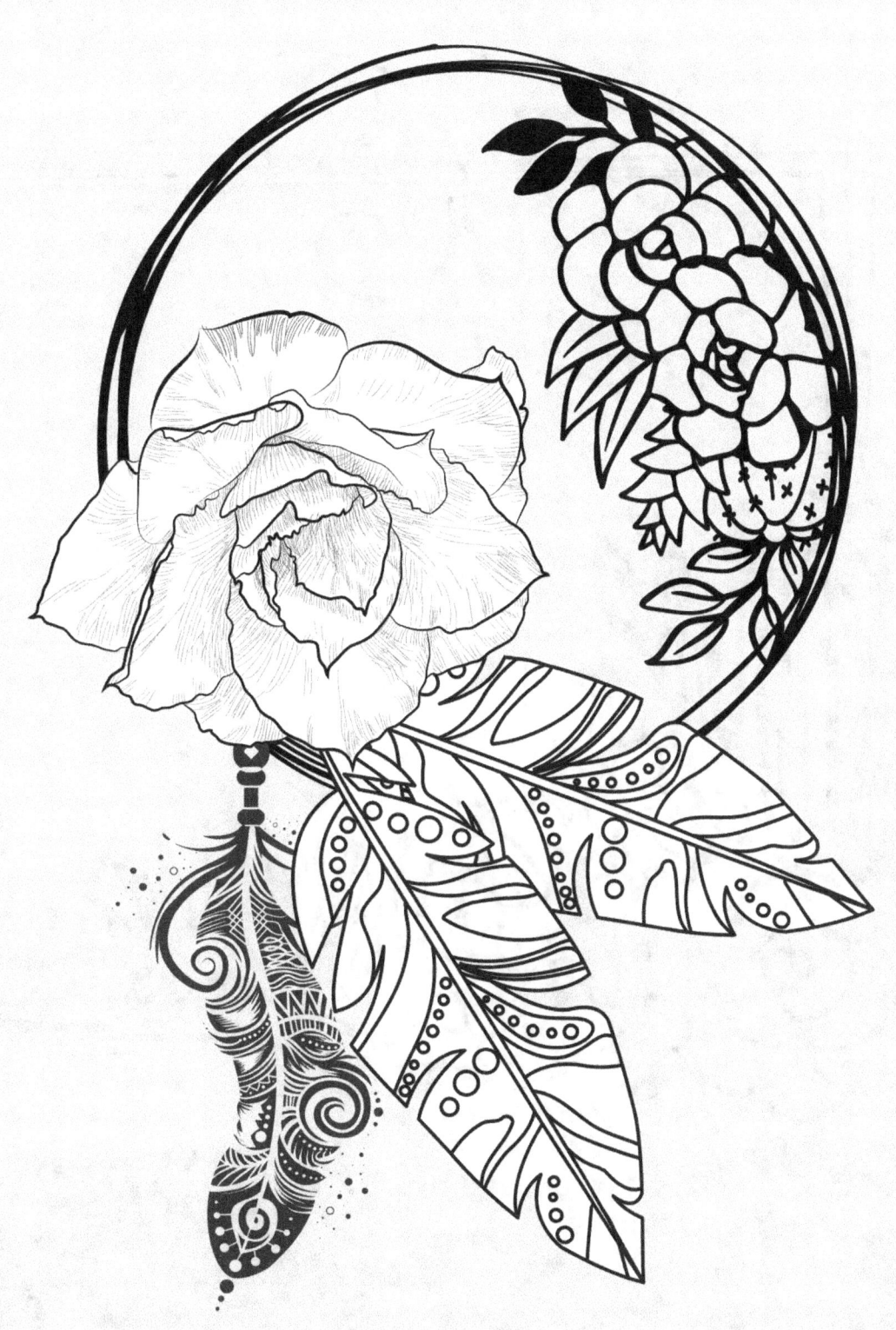

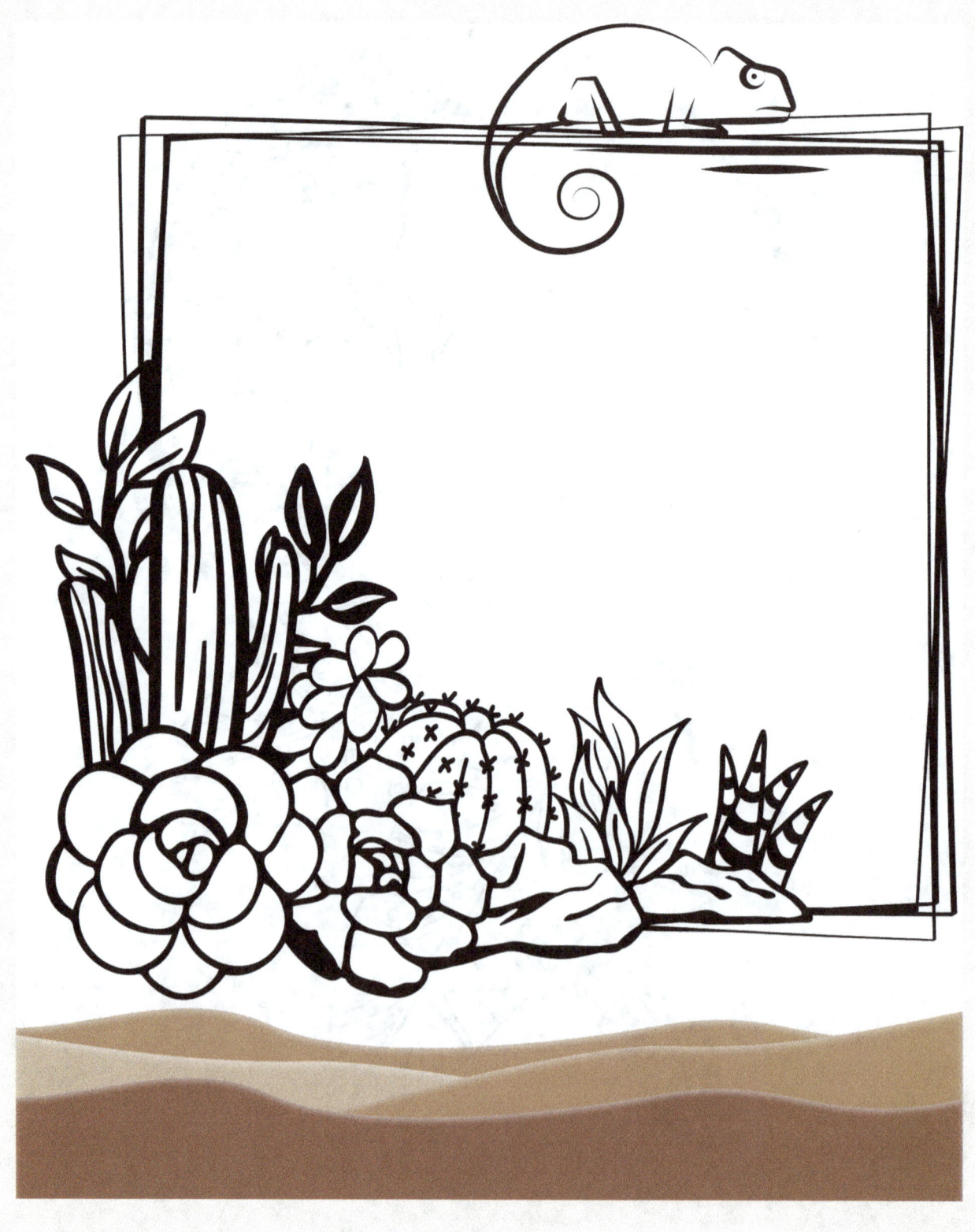

A Quick Thought

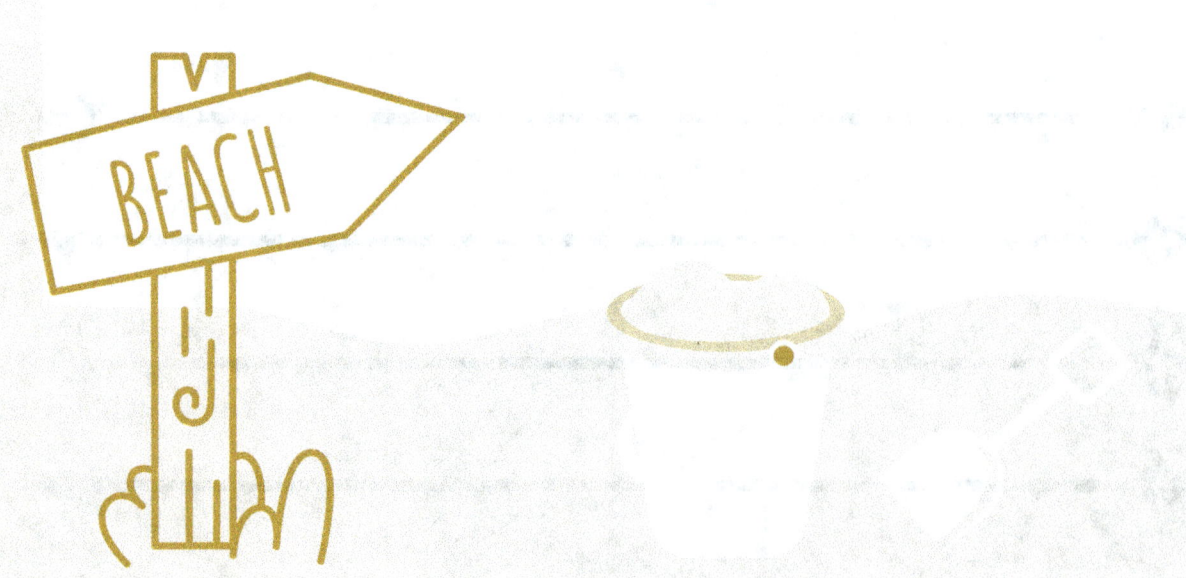

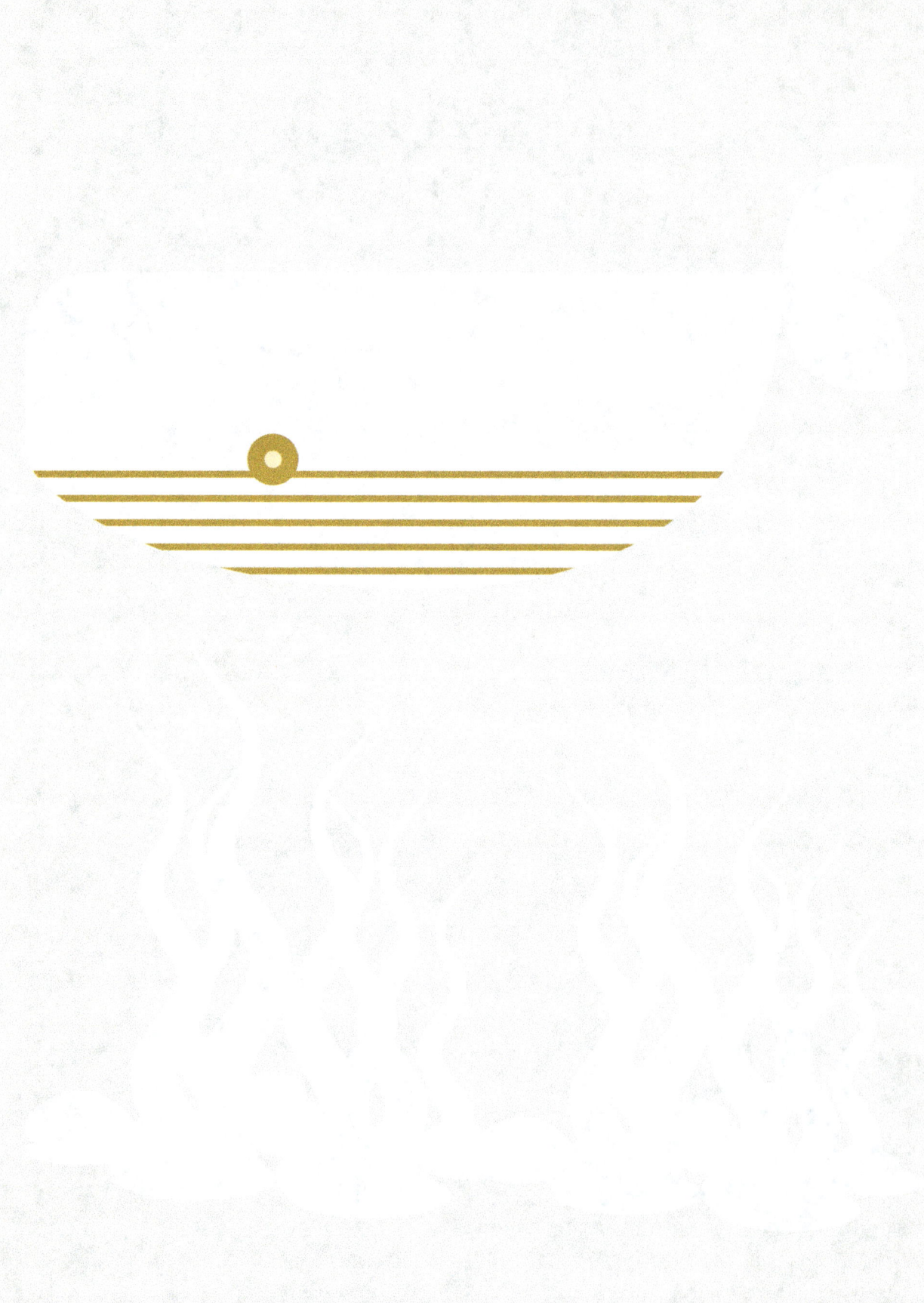

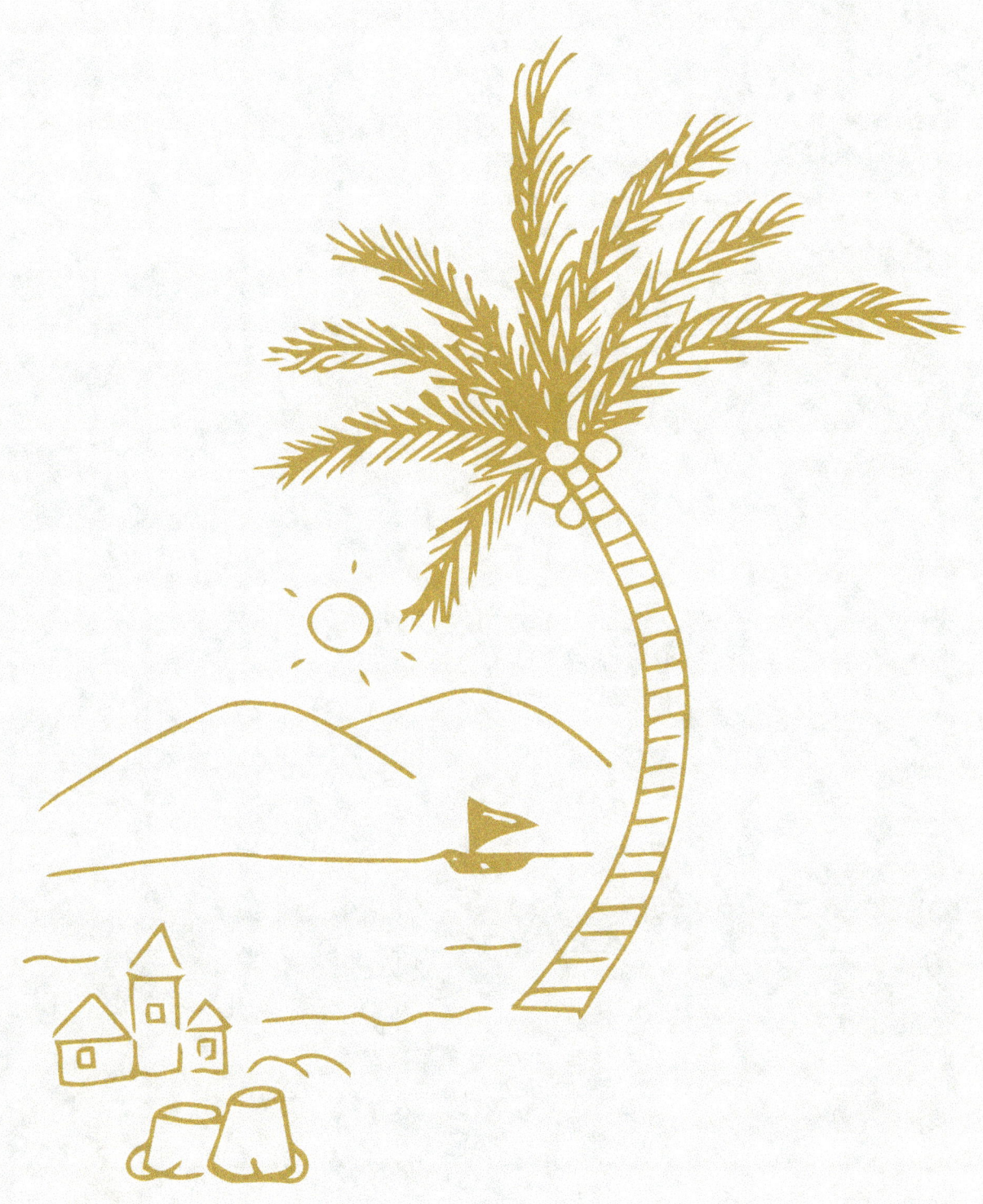

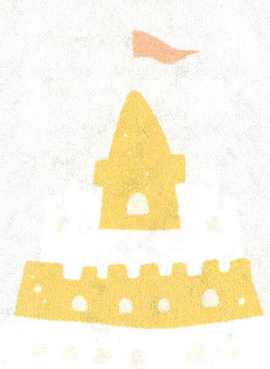

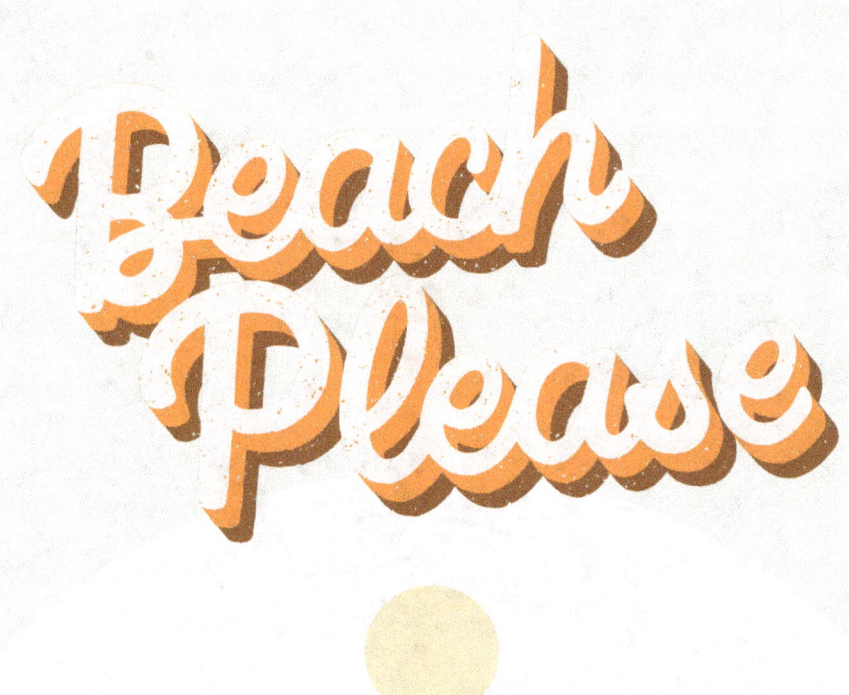

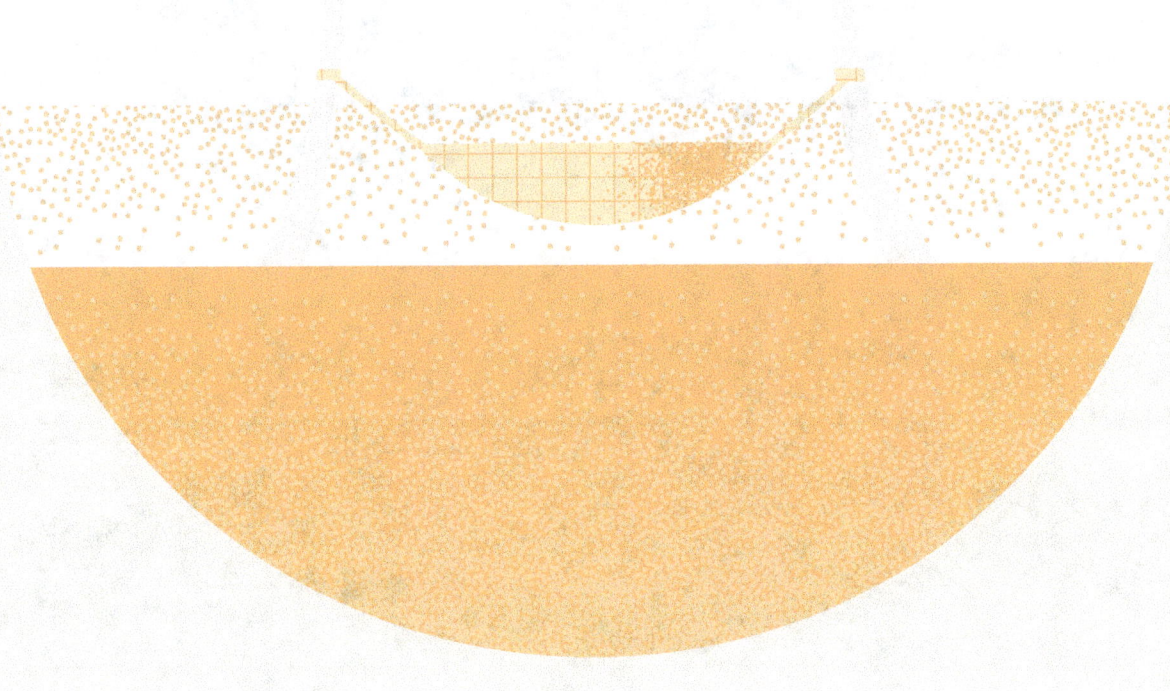

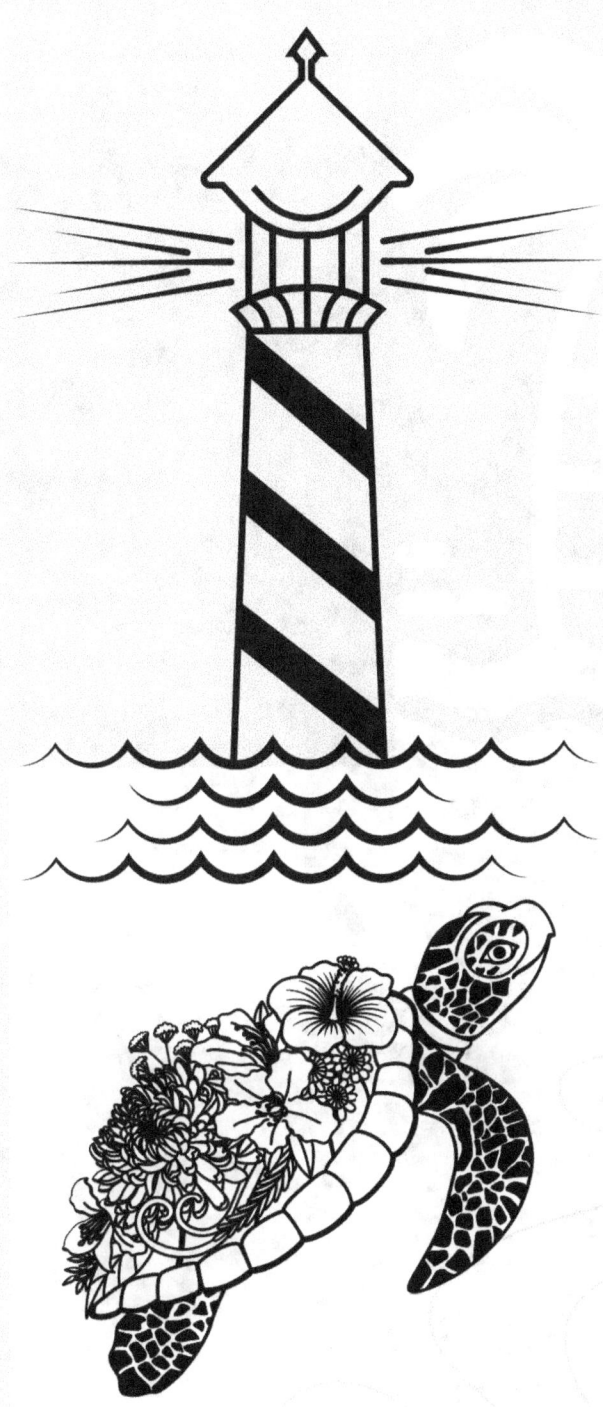

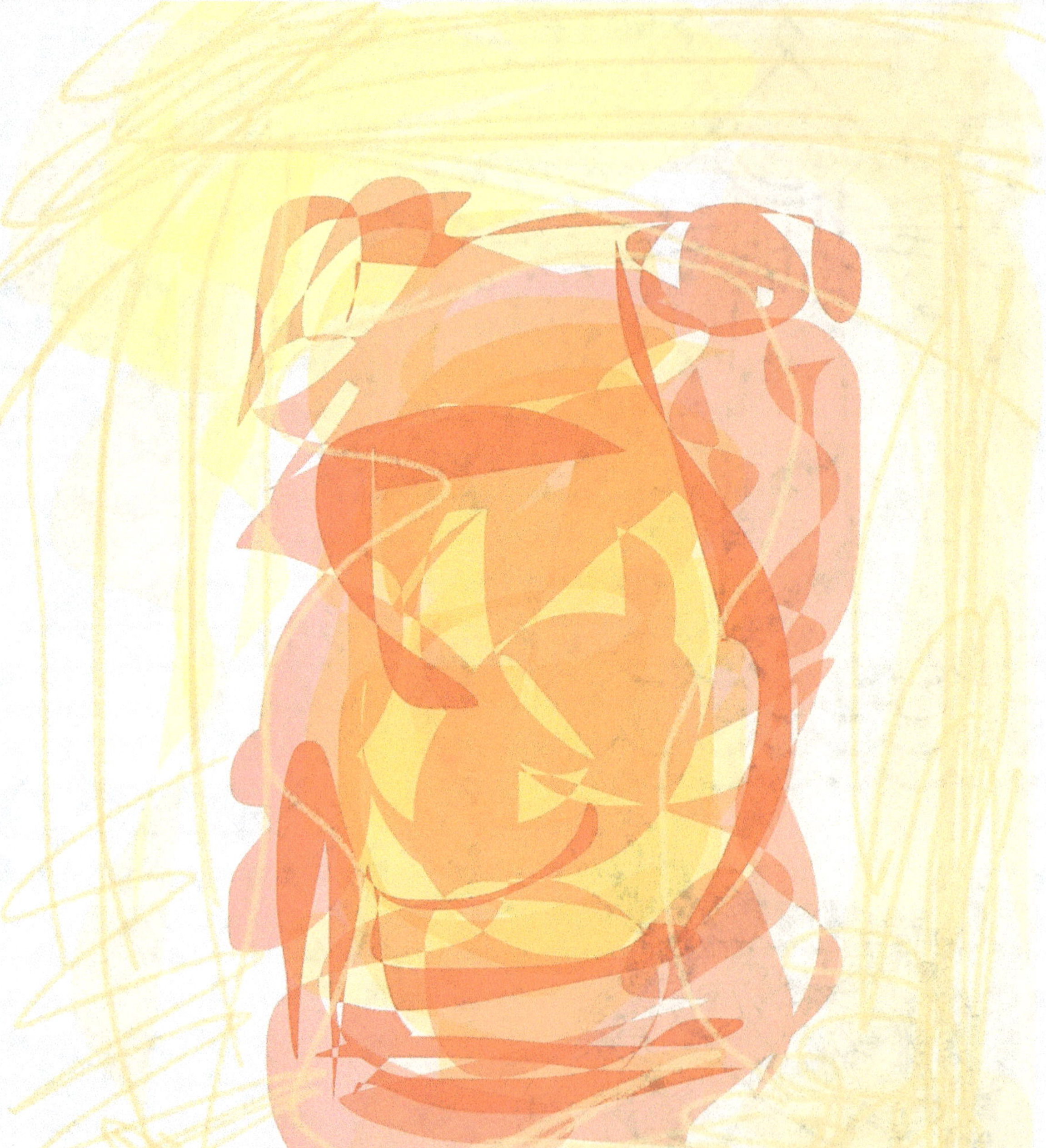

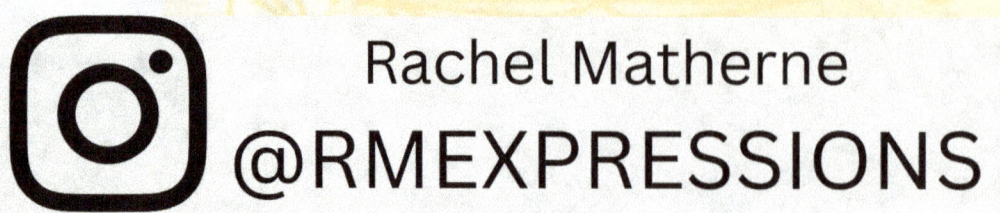

Rachel Matherne
@RMEXPRESSIONS

www.ingramcontent.com/pod-product-compliance
Lightning Source LLC
Chambersburg PA
CBHW080856220526
45467CB00008B/2525